ARSEN*

GREATS

Dedications

I would like to dedicate this book to two generations of Arsenal supporters — to my father Ted, 75 years young, and to my son, Ben, aged 8.

My father, a lifelong Arsenal fan, filled my head as a lad with stories of his beloved Gunners.

Nothing will ever make him change his mind that the Arsenal attack in the early Thirties of Hulme-Jack-Lambert-James-Bastin was the greatest forward line in British soccer history.

He showed me the light and I have tried to do likewise for my son, Ben.

Judging by the pictures of 'Rocky', Michael Thomas, Alan Smith, Paul Merson and Tony Adams etc., etc., etc. on his bedroom wall, I think I can safely assume that, like his dad and his grandad, he's well and truly hooked!

ARSENAL GREATS

Keith Fisher

Foreword by

George Graham
Manager of Arsenal F.C.

SPORTSPRINT PUBLISHING
EDINBURGH

© Keith Fisher 1990

All rights reserved.

No part of this publication may be reproduced
in any form or by any means without
the prior permission of the publishers,
John Donald Publishers Ltd.,
138 St Stephen Street, Edinburgh EH3 5AA

ISBN 0 85976 314 5

British Library Cataloguing in Publication Data
Fisher, Keith
 Arsenal greats.
 1. Association football — Biographies — collections
 I. Title
 796.334092

Phototypeset by Beecee Typesetting Services
Printed and bound in Great Britain by Bell & Bain Ltd., Glasgow

Foreword

I am delighted to be writing this foreword to Keith Fisher's book on 'Arsenal Greats'.

I'm even more delighted that he has included me among them!

Seriously, it is a great honour to be considered alongside men such as Alex James, Cliff Bastin, Frank McLintock, Joe Mercer and Liam Brady. They've all played such a significant part in Arsenal's history.

I've known Keith Fisher since his days as a young sports journalist on the *Sunday Mirror*. I had just finished my playing career and was contemplating my next move in football.

We have both moved up in the world since then — me as manager of the famous Arsenal and Keith as Sports Editor of the *Daily Mirror*.

I may not always agree with him, but I know he has a genuine love for the Gunners.

It couldn't have been easy for Keith selecting the names for his book. There are so many great players to choose from.

I speak from experience — I was once landed with the unenviable job of picking the best Arsenal team in a special video promotion in 1989. What a sweat that turned out to be!

Yes, I think I know the nightmares Keith must have gone through before settling on his final choice of 'Arsenal Greats'.

George Graham
Manager
Arsenal FC

Acknowledgements

I am indebted to Len Greener, Picture Editor of the *Daily Mirror*, for his permission to raid the extensive MGN Library for photographs used in this book and my good friend and colleague Siggy Jacobsen for his painstaking efforts in choosing the right ones!

The photograph of George Graham, facing page 1, was taken by the *Daily Mirror*'s Arnold Slater, one of Fleet Street's top sports photographers. It is reproduced with his kind permission.

I must also thank George Graham for his Foreword and the players of Arsenal FC, past and present, whose skills and endeavours in that famous red-and-white shirt have provided me with so many wonderful memories. Thanks, lads.

Last, but not least, my task was made a lot easier with the knowledge gained from *Arsenal 1886-1986* by Phil Soar and Martin Tyler. It is the official Centenary history of the club.

Contents

The Legend of Herbert Chapman

HOW ELSE COULD I INTRODUCE THIS BOOK OF Arsenal 'Greats' other than with the man who introduced greatness to Arsenal?

Without Herbert Chapman, the famous Gunners might be just another ordinary soccer club content in mid-table anonymity, instead of a national institution and a name synonymous with world football.

For the benefit of the younger reader or for those who have led a sheltered life, the legendary Chapman's era belonged to the roaring Thirties when Arsenal conquered all. But Chapman wasn't just about results. His greatness was that he established the very traditions, style and integrity upon which this most famous club has been built.

Bernard Joy, an outstanding old centre-half who retained his amateur status right through his distinguished Arsenal career, called Chapman: 'The greatest manager the game has ever seen — without any doubt.'

Joy, an England international and later to become one of the most knowledgeable and respected journalists in Fleet Street, went on: 'Herbert Chapman lifted League football to a professional level and helped turn it into a great entertainment industry. He knew tactics backwards and got players to lift themselves to new levels.

'He encouraged ideas from every member of his staff —

from apprentice, tea lady, right through to the most famous of internationals. Also, he had such a marvellous flair for publicity.

'He realised instantly the attraction of having an Underground station right on Arsenal's doorstep. So, after months of negotiation with the relevant bodies, he persuaded them to change its name from Gillespie Road to Arsenal. In doing so, the name of Arsenal was on the map for the whole of London to see.

'Chapman was 20 years ahead of his time — he advocated the introduction of floodlights, numbers on the backs of players' jerseys and even artificial pitches.

'Herbert Chapman was unique.'

This mood is endorsed by another Arsenal stalwart, the long-serving George Male.

He says: 'Mr Chapman was the greatest psychologist in the game. He could get you to do anything.'

As a permanent reminder of Chapman's influence on the history and status of Arsenal, his famous bust stands in splendid isolation in the marble foyer just inside the entrance to the East Stand.

It was the idea of twelve of Chapman's closest friends, including the man who eventually inherited his empire, Tom Whittaker. The bust was modelled by the famous sculptor Jacob Epstein.

Herbert Chapman was a Yorkshireman born in the small mining village of Kiveton Park.

An ordinary footballer, it is ironic to discover that his longest spell with one club was at Spurs, of all places. He spent two years at White Hart Lane — often as the butt of the boo-boys — as an insignificant, tubby little inside-forward before he took on his first managerial post at Northampton Town.

Chapman returned to his native Yorkshire to manage Leeds City before the club were thrown out of the Football League after making illegal payments to players, although Chapman was not at the club when the offences took place.

THE legendary Herbert Chapman. According to Bernard Joy he was 'the greatest manager the game has ever seen.'

In 1920, Chapman became manager of Huddersfield Town and immediately he began to weave his special brand of magic.

So much so that within three years Town became League Champions.

In May 1925 came the decision that was to change the face of Arsenal — and the course of its history.

Chapman, already a household name after his feats for Huddersfield, was approached by Arsenal chairman Henry

Norris and reportedly offered £2,000-a-year to put Arsenal on the map.

It was a challenge Chapman could not resist.

One of his first moves concerned the ever-faithful Tom Whittaker whose healing hands were soon to become part of soccer's folklore.

Injury had forced Whittaker into premature retirement and, on his return from an F.A. international tour, he was summoned by Chapman.

They walked to the top of the Arsenal North Bank terracing — then uncovered — before Chapman, spreading his arms wide towards the pitch, issued these immortal words:

'Tom, I'm going to make Arsenal the most famous club in soccer — and I'm going to make you the greatest trainer!'

Whittaker was hooked and together they formed a partnership that would take the world by storm.

So what sort of man was Chapman?

Bernard Joy, in his magnificent book *Forward Arsenal!* described him thus: 'There are two kinds of visionary; those that dream of a whole new world, and those who dream of just one thing. Chapman's vision was of the greatest football team in the world. His genius was in actually creating something close to that.'

Cliff Bastin, the most famous of all Arsenal wingers, didn't beat about the bush when he said: 'Herbert Chapman should have been Prime Minister!'

Chapman was all things — authoritarian and disciplinarian. He was totally committed to Arsenal's cause and ruthless in its execution. He was single-minded and outspoken. Yet he was fair.

He insisted — no, demanded — that everything about Arsenal should be first class. And he meant EVERYTHING — travel, hotels, meals, training facilities. Nothing was too good for Arsenal and its footballers. Consequently, the players were made to feel ten feet tall.

Above all, his personality radiated such an aura of

greatness — and fear — that lesser mortals felt completely overawed in his presence.

His philosophy was a simple one. He believed that great players made great football teams.

He was also a man who was never satisfied — a perfectionist who would never tolerate complacency.

Winger Joe Hulme once asked to spend a weekend in his native Lancashire after Arsenal's fixture at Burnden Park, Bolton.

'If we do well and if you do well, I'll think about it and let you know,' he told Hulme.

Arsenal won 5-0 with Hulme scoring two goals.

After the match Hulme looked at Chapman and said: 'Am I okay now for the weekend, boss?'

Chapman replied: 'Certainly not — you're playing for the third team at Highbury on Wednesday.'

Crestfallen, Hulme said: 'What! After scoring two goals this afternoon?'

Chapman countered: What about the three you missed.' Joe returned to London!

On another occasion Arsenal beat Wolves 7-1 at Molineux. In the team conference at Highbury the following Monday, Chapman tore the players apart for almost two hours . . . for conceding a goal!

Chapman set himself such high standards and expected everybody at the club to follow them.

After Arsenal had been beaten 2-0 by Walsall in the Third Round of the F.A. Cup in 1933 — still the biggest shock in the history of the Cup — Chapman sacked a young footballer called Tommy Black for kicking a Walsall player, conceding a penalty and getting his marching orders.

On the train back to London he instructed that Tommy should be sent home and never return to Highbury.

Chapman would tolerate nobody who discredited the great name of Arsenal Football Club.

Chapman knew every trick in the book and used it to Arsenal's advantage.

Famous Arsenal secretary Bob Wall, perhaps the man who knew Chapman best after working with him as his personal assistant, recalled in his book *Arsenal From The Heart*:

'A few months after I joined the staff of Arsenal Football Club, Chapman summoned me to his office.

'Young Wall, come with me today. I'll show you how to conduct a transfer,' he said.

'We are going to sign David Jack, the England inside-forward, from Bolton Wanderers. We are meeting their chairman and manager at the Euston Hotel. You are to sit with me, listen and not say a word. I'll do all the talking. Is that clear?

'We arrived at the hotel half-an-hour before our appointment. Chapman immediately went into the lounge bar. He called the waiter, placed two pound notes in his hand and said: 'George, this is Mr Wall, my assistant. He will drink whisky and dry ginger. I will drink gin and tonic. We shall be joined by guests. They will drink whatever they like. But I want you to be careful of one thing. See that our guests are given DOUBLE of everything. But Mr Wall's whisky and dry ginger will contain no whisky and my gin and tonic will contain no gin.'

'When the Bolton pair arrived, Chapman ordered the drinks. We quickly downed ours and he called for the same again. The drinks continued to flow and our friends were soon in a gay mood.

'Finally, when Chapman decided the time was opportune for talking business, they readily agreed to letting him sign Jack — and for £10,890 which we considered a bargain.

'Never did ginger ale and tonic water leave two persons so elated. When we were safely in our taxi on the return journey to Highbury, Chapman exclaimed: 'Wall, that's your first lesson in football. You now know how to conduct a transfer!'

'Chapman knew that Bolton did not want to sell David Jack. They had circulated clubs stating they had players on offer but Jack was not among them.

'The fee Chapman paid was the first five-figure transfer in the history of the game and the whole affair provided a fascinating glimpse of the acumen and personality of this remarkable man.

'No member of staff was allowed to leave Highbury unless he had telephoned Chapman's office at six o'clock and enquired: 'It is all right to leave, Mr Chapman?'

'We all had a very real respect for him. He was a great man. If he put up a scheme, you'd be willing to follow him to the end of the earth to ensure its fulfilment. You always felt that what he said was right.

'He never thought of himself. Arsenal FC was his creed. He was a hard, yet scrupulously fair person to staff and players and he remained constant in his attitudes until he died.

'Chapman had this extraordinary flair for revitalising anything he touched. He transformed Arsenal.'

Chapman left Huddersfield to join Arsenal a year before the Yorkshire club completed its hat-trick of League titles — the first club ever to do so.

In his first season at Highbury, Arsenal were runners-up in the First Division.

In 1927, the Gunners reached their first ever F.A. Cup Final, going down 0-1 to Cardiff City — a match in which the shiny new jersey of goalkeeper Dan Lewis cost Arsenal dear as the ball spun off his chest and into the net. So the coveted F.A. Cup went out of England for the only time in its history.

In 1930, Arsenal won the F.A. Cup for the first time, ironically against Chapman's old club Huddersfield. Arsenal were captained by Tom Parker.

In 1931, Arsenal were crowned Champions of the First Division for the first time and a year later became runners-up in both League and Cup.

In 1933, Chapman achieved the first leg of a Championship treble which tragically he did not live to see completed.

In January, 1934 he caught a chill while watching a midweek League match between Sheffield United and Birmingham.

Wall recalled: 'He travelled back to London overnight and though we prevailed upon him to go home to bed, he insisted on watching the third team play in a bitingly cold wind at Guildford.

'I haven't seen the boys for a week or so,' he said. 'This is a good opportunity.'

'He even ignored the advice of Dr Guy Pepper, the club doctor.'

Chapman returned home to Hendon feeling much worse and went to bed. He died of pneumonia in the early hours of the following Saturday morning — at 3 a.m. He was only 55.

Four days later on January 10, 1934, Chapman was buried at Hendon.

Chapman left behind a team that many argue was the greatest club side in the history of British soccer. They were all handpicked by a man of such charisma that he became a legend in his own lifetime.

From Frank Moss in goal to George Male and Eddie Hapgood at full back; from Herbie Roberts (the first 'stopper' centre-half in English football) to wee Alex James and David Jack at inside-forward; and from Joe Hulme on the right wing to Cliff Bastin on the left, Arsenal were THE team, dominating an era in such spectacular style that they will never be forgotten even when Arsenal celebrate their 200th anniversary in the year 2086.

No one has more vividly captured the magic of Arsenal created by Chapman than Geoffrey Green, Britain's most distinguished Soccer correspondent, who so tragically passed away in May, 1990 leaving a void never to be filled.

For over fifty years his words released marvellous images of the beautiful game for his army of readers in *The Times*.

The doyen of all soccer writers, Geoffrey wrote of Arsenal:

'When one speaks or writes the name of Arsenal there is an uncomfortable feeling that it should be done standing up.

'Loved or hated fiercely as they have been across the years

CHAPMAN jokes with the long-serving Bob John and the great Alex James.

there is still an unmistakeable ring about that name. It is a royal salute by gunfire.

'It was on the open north terrace at Highbury in the winter of 1929 that my eyes were first opened to the magic and poetry of football.

'I had always loved the game from my earliest youth. But in one sudden moment that wet afternoon long ago the sheer wonder of it struck home. It was done in a twinkling.

'Sheffield United were the visitors. They opened the scoring early on. Then came the lightning. The blinding flash was provided by wee Alex James, the genius, recently arrived from the north.

'As a fast through pass out of defence cut down the middle, James flitted across its line, waved a foot over the ball letting it go on its path unhindered.

'The full effect was achieved without so much as a touch. It was like the waving of a conjuror's wand.

'The whole Sheffield defence was mesmerised and wrong-footed; a wide avenue opened up like magic and through it strolled Lambert with the ball to stroke home the equaliser.

'From that moment the Yorkshiremen were cut to pieces as Arsenal swept gloriously to an 8-1 victory. Yet all that my memory still hugs is that feint, that decoy by James. It was the beginning of an education.

'Soon after that the name of Arsenal went around the world. They became as famous in Finland, in Greenland, in Chile, in China, as in north London.

'Clubs, even small amateur growths in hamlets, copied their red colours.

'They became a byword as team after team, even national sides overseas, imitated — or tried to — their new defensive system of the stopper centre-half invented in 1926 by Herbert Chapman, their famous manager, and Charles Buchan, their reigning captain, to counter the recent change in the offside law.

'It was Herbert Chapman who became the true architect of the Arsenal of modern times.

'Having earlier made Huddersfield Town the colossus of English football, he now achieved the trick at Highbury so that he became the master tactician and the dominating single link between the 1920s and 1930s.

'Yet by their very domination of those great days Arsenal aroused a mountain of jealousy in small minded people.

'The North, in particular, found its nose put out of joint. "Lucky Arsenal" became the parrot cry as the suspicion grew that here were merely the nouveau riche of a changing world, living on cheap publicity.

'How the years have proved them all wrong! There have been good times since those days, but many bad times, too. Yet Arsenal have proved themselves, through thick and thin, no bubble to be easily pricked.

'Over seven decades in an ocean of time to remain bouyant in the pressure-cooker of modern football, where success usually has lasted only over midnight and where new idols swiftly take the place of the old.

'Whatever the raging, endless arguments over comparisons — one thing remains.

'Even mere utility is granted a special quality by the Arsenal tradition, a quality that still keeps the club its glorious and hard won position in the opinions of those who must face it.

'Part of this tradition is that seldom does a man who joins Highbury want to leave. That in itself is significant.

'Arsenal today remain a monument, one of the prides of the capital, a place where millions have made their pilgrimage.'

The last word on Chapman goes to Bob Wall: 'Several times a season, for a number of years after his death I, and indeed, other members of the staff heard footsteps in the corridors of Highbury Stadium as we worked late in the evening.

'The steps would tap their progress along the upper landing from the gymnasium, through the boardroom, past my door, through the cocktail bar, onto the Press room and right down the stand. They were the same measured footsteps as Herbert Chapman's which I came to know so well as a young man.

'Sometimes, at the sound of walking, I would open my office door and look down the passage.

'I never saw anything. All that I — and the rest of the office staff — ever heard were those measured steps. If they belonged to Herbert Chapman, then I'm sure he must have been there for a very good purpose!'

So Herbert Chapman was the man who inspired the Arsenal story for future generations of players, managers and supporters.

What follows in this book, then, is a personal selection of Arsenal 'Greats' — both past and present.

When I first arrived into the big, bright world of sports journalism I was told that the 'art of editing is not what you put in, but it is what you leave out.'

There have been so many great players from great teams in Arsenal's long, distinguished history that I can only apologise for those 'Greats' who didn't make it here. I hope you enjoy this book as much as I did compiling it.

CHAPTER 1

George Graham

TALL, DARK AND HANDSOME, GEORGE GRAHAM breezed into Anfield like a soccer giant on that fateful night of Friday, May 26, 1989 when a Football League Championship had reached its climax.

And with his customary ice-cool, confident manner, masterminded a victory for Arsenal that nobody in their right frame of mind could possibly have envisaged.

To gauge the significance of that historic occasion you have to recall the background, build-up and the very special atmosphere that preceded the greatest soccer night I can ever recall — and will never forget.

Arsenal had casually, almost ridiculously, blown a 17-point advantage over their Merseyside rivals that had seen them toppled from the No. 1 spot they had held since Boxing Day. Liverpool, meanwhile, in their relentless pursuit of a title they had regarded as their very own over the last decade, had moved ominously into pole position.

The tragedy of Hillsborough when 95 people lost their lives — crushed to death on the Leppings Lane terracing during an F.A. Cup semi-final with Nottingham Forest — had affected not just football folk but a society that was suddenly made horribly aware of the terrible way spectators are treated at soccer stadia up and down the country.

So the whole wide world, aware that a new responsibility was needed, put their hearts firmly behind Kenny Dalglish and a red army of footballers who had behaved with tremendous dignity after soccer's greatest tragedy.

JUBILATION as Graham hugs assistant-manager Theo Foley after victory at Anfield.

A 3-2 F.A. Cup Final victory over fierce Merseyside rivals Everton had thrilled millions all around the world — and all that was left to complete a unique Double was the expected demolition of Arsenal in the final game of the season.

How fitting that this dramatic finale should conclude the first season of ITV's exclusive live contract with the Football League! Things could not have worked out more favourably if they had written the script themselves.

I've been an Arsenal 'nut' since my father first built a small wooden stool for me to stand on to enable me to poke my nose over the Arsenal railings on the famous North Bank so many years ago.

Yet I didn't think Arsenal stood an earthly. I thought the Gunners had blown it that previous week after a crushing 2-1 defeat by Derby County on the Saturday and then dropping two points against lowly Wimbledon the following Tuesday.

However, it had been a great season for Arsenal and as I applauded the players on their customary lap of honour after

GRAHAM, Championship trophy in one hand, acknowledges the cheers at Anfield.

the 2-2 draw with the Dons I prayed for the miracle that I thought was needed to bring the Championship trophy back to Highbury for the first time since 1971.

I obviously reckoned without George Graham's powers of motivation.

If there was one man who remained convinced that Arsenal Football Club could climb an Everest and beat Liverpool 2-0, that man was clearly the tall, elegant Bargeddie-born Scotsman whose love affair with Arsenal began with his £80,000 transfer from London neighbours Chelsea in 1966 — a deal that involved Tommy Baldwin going to Stamford Bridge as a makeweight.

The result may be history now but who can ever forget George Graham's finest hour?

There are those who subscribe to the view that Liverpool played beneath themselves that night — content to sit on a goalless draw or even a 1-0 defeat that would enable them to keep their title.

It is a view that I dismiss completely. Arsenal swamped

THE smile says it all — and George still won't let go of the trophy!

Liverpool with a determination and belief in their football that was nothing short of breathtaking.

Liverpool didn't lose the most important match of the season — Arsenal won it because they outplayed their Mersey-side rivals. Simple as that.

And the man responsible, George Graham, had been the

STICK it in the family album! George with son Daniel and daughter Nicole after the Anfield triumph.

architect of the most astonishing title-race cliff-hanger in the history of the League Championship.

From the minute he walked into Anfield, George believed totally in Arsenal's destiny. So much so that Arsenal skipper Tony Adams recalls: 'The boss, in the way that he handled the team, made us believe we were going to do it. He was incredible. We couldn't wait to get out there. We felt like supermen.'

The man himself was certain. 'Yes, we have a mountain to climb,' he answered when the Press sought his views before the game, 'but we can do it. I believe so, my players believe so.'

After the game, clinched by Arsenal in injury-time by Michael Thomas's goal, George posed for the posse of photographers — wearing the smile of a man who knew his work had been done.

George, meticulous George, had planned, plotted and finally perfected surely Arsenal's greatest-ever triumph.

So Graham became only the fifth manager in Arsenal's magnificent 103-year history to claim a League Championship — following in the footsteps of the legendary Chapman, George Allison, Tom Whittaker and Bertie Mee.

There are those Arsenal fans who may question George's right to be included ahead of Whittaker and Mee in this book of Arsenal 'Greats'. A controversial choice? Perhaps.

But, after his achievement against all the odds at Anfield, I had no hesitation. And there are few people who would doubt that it is just the start of a golden new era of success for the Gunners.

Not forgetting, of course, that George was one of the most influential players in Arsenal's epic League and Cup Double of 1971.

For me, the combination of outstanding player and then outstanding manager is irresistible.

It is a photograph of Chapman alongside those of Allison, Whittaker and Mee which holds pride of place in Graham's study at his North London home.

It is that photograph of the man who unfolded the Arsenal legend in the Thirties which George gazes at daily to remind him of the traditions Chapman established in the foundation of Arsenal Football Club.

Although George remains a very private man in his own private world — outsiders very rarely break his tough exterior — the club's traditions mean everything to him.

For once freeing himself from his natural inhibitions, George spoke fluently and eloquently about previous managers on the run-in to Arsenal's victory at Liverpool.

'I have my own dream,' he said. 'A dream to join the greats of Arsenal. To put my picture on my study wall alongside Chapman, Mee, Allison and Whittaker. To make it myself into my own Arsenal Hall of Fame as manager of a League Championship-winning side. It means everything to me.

HE'S still smiling! This time in front of Arsenal's fans at the club's Civic Reception at Islington Town Hall.

'I look at the photographs I have of these special men and I want to be alongside them. That is why I wanted to become manager of Arsenal. That is how I want to be remembered — with legends from Arsenal's past and me as Arsenal's future.'

Emotional words. It is timely to talk of Bertie Mee, the man who masterminded the famous Double season in 1971. An ordinary little winger briefly with Derby County, his superb work in physiotherapy at a Camden Town rehabilitation clinic first clinched his career at Highbury.

Mee went on to claim his own special place in the Arsenal Hall of Fame when, to the astonishment of the soccer world, he was asked by chairman Denis Hill-Wood to succeed the disappointing Billy Wright as Arsenal boss in 1966.

Bertie built a superb Arsenal team in which George Graham was his very first signing. And so we have George Graham the footballer — and a great one at that, eventually!

Yet his arrival at Arsenal with a reputation as a free-scoring centre-forward — 25 goals for Chelsea under Tommy

Docherty in 1964 — soon led to disappointment among the fans when he failed to blossom as the striker upon whom Mee would build his new attack.

In an Arsenal team going through a transitional period, George struggled to recapture his early scoring form with Chelsea.

But new coach Don Howe was soon to completely reshape the career of the Scot and, ultimately, provide Arsenal with a midfield player of extravagant elegance.

Howe, a splendid England full-back with West Bromwich Albion, had arrived at Arsenal in the autumn of his career — bought by the hapless Wright for a fee of £40,000 in 1964.

A broken leg 70 games into his career at Highbury signalled the end, and a switch to the coaching staff followed.

It is to Mee's eternal credit that when Dave Sexton quit Arsenal to become manager of Chelsea he had no hesitation in plumping for the enthusiastic Black Countryman to fill the void.

It proved Mee's finest appointment as slowly, but surely, they assembled a team to take Arsenal back to their rightful place at the pinnacle of English soccer.

Massive disappointments in two Football League Cup Finals — 0-1 to Leeds United in a dour, defensive game at Wembley in 1968, and public humiliation at the hands of Third Division Swindon Town in 1969 — were a prelude to victory in the old European Fairs Cup in 1970 and that momentous Double a year later.

Sharing those tragedies and triumphs was George. Howe had quickly discovered that the Scot's silky skills were better suited to a more withdrawn role in midfield, and how his game blossomed!

Although he was brilliant in the air, George was never a great goalscorer. However, from midfield he became a scorer of great goals in his 300-plus appearances in that famous red and white shirt.

One that will always spring to mind came in the replayed F.A. Cup semi-final with Stoke City at Villa Park in March

THE best of enemies — George and Tottenham manager Terry Venables.

1971 when he scored Arsenal's first goal with a header of classical proportions.

Arsenal's supporters will undoubtedly choose their own 'George special' because there were certainly enough of them.

It was during these triumphant days that Graham's head became swelled with the traditions and emotions of belonging to Arsenal, but when Bertie Mee paid £200,000 — then a British record — for Everton's Alan Ball at Christmas, 1971 the writing was on the wall. George was to last one more season.

Ironically, it was Graham's former boss Tommy Docherty who rescued his career when, in 1972, he paid Arsenal £120,000 to sign him for Manchester United.

It was to be a brief reunion as Graham's career was clearly on the wane, and downmarket moves to Portsmouth, QPR and Crystal Palace confirmed the end.

It was at homely Selhurst Park in South London under his great pal Terry Venables — his best man at his wedding in 1967 — that the seeds were first sown on a new career in coaching. Either that or opening a pub!

Graham's first steps on the managerial merry-go-round came when he took up a difficult, challenging job at Millwall, a club with one of the worst hooligan records in soccer.

But he threw himself into the task, did the impossible by promoting a softer, friendlier image for the Docklands club and even won promotion to the Second Division. Graham was winning rave reviews up and down the country — a young man clearly destined for a big job at a big club.

Then, in the summer of 1986, came the call to Highbury he was waiting for — to replace, of all people, Don Howe — the man who had been responsible for rescuing his playing career. George had made it.

But it was a different George Graham who returned to Highbury — gone was the old, casual, elegant 'stroller' image and in its place a disciplined tough guy eager to sort out the indiscipline that had eaten away at Arsenal's proud image over the previous few years.

George made it known he was the guv'nor in every sense of the word — clearing out those he considered troublesome players and giving Arsenal's exciting crop of teenagers their chance.

His first words were prophetic: 'I am proud to be Arsenal's manager. Nobody loves this club more than me. I'll get it right. And if I can achieve the sort of success I had here as a player, then I'll be a happy man.'

In his first season in charge — 1986-87 — George won the Littlewoods Cup at Wembley, beating Liverpool 2-1 (funny how that name keeps cropping up!).

In his second season, he again won through to the Little-woods Cup Final at Wembley — this time going down 3-2 to Luton Town in a marvellously entertaining match.

But those two years had been spent applying the finishing touches to a side not dissimilar in style to the Double team in preparation for an assault on the League Championship in season 1988-89.

And it was all done with George's record outlay in the

THE brains behind Arsenal collects an Honorary Fellowship at North London Polytechnic for leading the Gunners to glory in 1989.

transfer market being the £750,000 he paid Leicester for the tall, gangling Alan Smith.

In an era of spend, spend, spend, George has proved conclusively that you don't need the cheque-book philosophy to bring back success to a club — but don't tell that to Terry Venables at Spurs or Alex Ferguson at Manchester United!

Graham, manager of one of the wealthiest, most stable clubs in the First Division, has followed such a policy with extravagant success.

His Championship-winning squad included six players he signed from smaller clubs for a total of £1.8 million:

Brian Marwood from Sheffield Wednesday: £500,000.

Steve Bould from Stoke City: £350,000.

Lee Dixon from Stoke: £350,000.

Nigel Winterburn from Wimbledon: £350,000.

Kevin Richardson from Watford: £150,000.

Perry Groves from Colchester: £65,000.

And in just 12 golden months George made Arsenal the richest club in the country. They pulled in a staggering £5 million for winning the League Championship, the World Club Championship in Miami, Florida; the British Championship in Glasgow; and the pre-season Mercantile title at Wembley.

Add to that income from sponsorship and commercial activities plus the club's own money-spinning schemes and there was another £4 million to swell the kitty.

In effect, the Gunners overtook Liverpool as the team everybody wanted to see and the most commercially marketable.

Lee Walker, head of the Football League's commercial department, says: 'As far as box office is concerned Arsenal are top of the table.'

In summing up Arsenal's future George says: 'There are two hurdles we've got over and as far as I'm concerned there's only one still to come.

'The first was getting the right staff on and off the pitch, the second was to win a major trophy which we did in our first season. The third obstacle, and probably the most difficult, is to maintain that success over a period.

'The League Championship is just the start. I think the amount of work we're putting in should give us that lasting success.'

There are few Arsenal supporters who would doubt that.

GEORGE GRAHAM'S PLAYING RECORD

	LEAGUE		F.A. CUP		F.L. CUP		EUROPE		TOTAL	
	App	Gls	App	Gls	App	Gls	App	Gls	App	Gls
1966-67	33	11	4	1					37	12
1967-68	38	16	5		8	5			51	21
1968-69	26	4	1		5				31	4
1969-70	36	7	2		4	2	11	5	53	14
1970-71	38	11	6	1	5	1	8	1	57	14
1971-72	40	8	9		4	1	6	1	59	10
1972-73	16	2			3				19	2
	227	59	27	2	29	9	25	7	308	77

SCOTLAND: 1972 v Portugal, Holland, Northern Ireland, Yugoslavia, Czechoslovakia, Brazil; 1973 v Denmark (2) (8 caps).

CHAPTER 2

Kenny Sansom

THERE CAN BE NO HIGHER COMPLIMENT TO Kenny Sansom than that he should rate comparison with two of the game's biggest legends.

For Arsenal, the arguments will always rage as to whether the title of 'Arsenal's greatest ever left-back' should go to Sansom or Eddie Hapgood.

Hapgood, from Arsenal's golden era under manager Herbert Chapman in the Thirties, made 440 first-team appearances in 11 years and became a fixture as England's captain.

Older Arsenal supporters will tell you that there wasn't another full-back to touch him and, in those halcyon days alongside such greats as Alex James, Cliff 'Boy' Bastin, Joe Hulme and David Jack, Arsenal were simply unbeatable.

For England, Sansom was without doubt the best left-back for a decade — an astonishing achievement considering the wear and tear, pressures and commitment needed by today's players to remain at the very peak of their profession.

And it is for England that Sansom with 86 international caps (including 9 caps with Crystal Palace) is good enough to be judged alongside Ray Wilson, whom many claim is the finest left-back in England's soccer history.

Wilson, who started his career at Huddersfield before moving on to Everton, was England's left-back in that dramatic 4-2 victory over West Germany in the 1966 World Cup Final.

Sir Alf Ramsey, England's finest manager and the brains

SANSOM on the ball — for 10 years England's first-choice left-back.

behind that triumph, rated the skilful little Yorkshireman as 'truly world class'.

It speaks volumes for Sansom, then, that he should be considered in the same breath.

Arsenal's long, proud history has been littered with

quality left-backs but it was Sansom who got manager George Graham's vote in a video promotion in 1989 entitled 'The Greatest Ever Arsenal Team'.

Graham short-listed six players — Hapgood, Wally Barnes and Lionel Smith from the Fifties, Bob McNab and Sammy Nelson from the Seventies, and Kenny Sansom from the modern generation.

Here's how he rated them.

EDDIE HAPGOOD: 'Eddie was probably one of the best left-backs not just for Arsenal but for England, too, over a long, long spell. A true Arsenal man, he played up to the Second World War — and won many, many caps. Of course, I didn't see him play but I would love to have watched him. People who did tell me he was immaculate, classy and in the glory, glory days of the Thirties formed a tremendous full-back partnership with George Male.'

WALLY BARNES: 'He took over from Hapgood and proved a wonderful player for Arsenal.'

LIONEL SMITH: 'Another classy player who also won international honours for England while at Arsenal.'

BOB McNAB: 'A tremendous footballer who loved getting forward and as a defender was absolutely brilliant. Bob was a great professional with a tremendous attitude.'

SAMMY NELSON: 'He formed a superb full-back partnership with Pat Rice for both Arsenal and Northern Ireland. They had some great times together.'

KENNY SANSOM: 'I first played with Kenny at Crystal Palace when he was just 17 — then he got his big money move to Arsenal. Kenny was the best left-back in England for a decade — and is the most capped Arsenal footballer. He had a great left foot and a great attitude.'

Graham concluded: 'It was a very difficult choice choosing from so many quality players but I have no hesitation in going for Kenny Sansom as Arsenal's greatest ever left-back.'

MIRROR, mirror on the wall — who's the best defender of them all?

Rich praise, indeed, for the stylish, dapper little South Londoner who joined Arsenal in the most bizarre of transfers.

It is worthwhile to recall the background to a transfer that caused something of a sensation at the time.

In August 1980 then manager Terry Neill shocked the soccer world by paying £1 million to Queens Park Rangers for a 19-year-old scoring prodigy called Clive Allen. He was the son of Les, who older fans will remember helped Spurs to the Football League and F.A. Cup Double in 1961.

Young Allen was then only the fifth English player to cost that sort of money — the others being Trevor Francis (Birmingham to Nottingham Forest), Andy Gray (Aston Villa to Wolves), Steve Daley (Wolves to Manchester City), and Kevin Reeves (Norwich to Manchester City).

But before young Clive had played a single first-team game for the Gunners — he was transferred to Crystal Palace in exchange for Kenny Sansom with Highbury keeper Paul Barron a makeweight in the deal.

Immediately, people cried 'foul'. It was alleged that there

was bad blood between Rangers and Crystal Palace, then managed by Terry Venables.

Venables wanted desperately to sign Allen, but he had been turned down flat by Rangers.

Arsenal wanted Sansom, so a deal was hatched between the two managers . . . the Gunners sign Allen then sell him on in exchange for Sansom.

In reality, Arsenal with two dynamic strikers in Alan Sunderland and Frank Stapleton, had got it all wrong. In two months, Neill and his right-hand man Don Howe discovered Allen was not the future and with four Cup Finals already under their belt in the previous three seasons — F.A. Cup Finals in '78, '79, '80 and the European Cup Winners' Cup in '80 — exchanged him for the class of Sansom.

Looking back, Arsenal got the better of the deal — emphasised immediately by Sansom's sparkling debut for Arsenal against West Bromwich Albion at The Hawthorns in the first game of the 1980-81 season. His immaculate defensive play, allied to some superb attacking runs up that left flank, had the Arsenal supporters drooling in a 1-0 victory.

Sansom went on to star in the No. 3 jersey for Arsenal throughout the Eighties, amassing nearly 400 matches and, in all but a handful, hardly put that left foot wrong.

But being one of the world's finest full-backs was no compensation for the lack of success at club level.

A Second Division championship medal with Palace in 1979 was all he had to show for seasons of hard graft, sweat and toil. He was envious of England colleagues carrying off the game's top honours.

Arsenal, in transition after their great Cup exploits, merely flattered to deceive when it came to winning the big prizes.

In his book *Going Great Guns* Sansom recalled the frustration of those days.

He said: 'I was the England left-back, captain of Arsenal and yet I couldn't see myself winning a thing. In my first F.A.

'I'LL pot the Reds!' Sansom relaxes with his great pal, Graham Rix.

Cup tie for the club I put through my own goal at Everton and Arsenal were knocked out. As the frustration went on, it began to bug me.

'It all changed with the arrival of George Graham in season 1986-87 and with it Arsenal's first Cup Final since 1980.'

Sansom went on: 'In one of his first team talks the boss gave, he told us of his hopes for Arsenal. He wanted to make

SANSOM and manager Terry Neill after his transfer from Crystal Palace.

them great again, regain the reputation that the club had in the Seventies under Bertie Mee. It was music to my ears.'

There was a disappointing start to the new association as Arsenal and George Graham slowly came to terms with each other. Then came an unbeaten 22-match run which acted as a springboard to a marvellous campaign in the Littlewoods Cup highlighted by three titanic clashes with the old enemy Spurs in the semi-finals.

With Liverpool to overcome in the final hurdle at Wembley on Sunday, April 5, 1987, Sansom was now on the brink of his first major club honour.

Thanks to two Charlie Nicholas goals Sansom was there and he could hardly conceal his delight as he went up Wembley's famous Royal Steps to collect the Cup in Arsenal's Centenary Year.

He said: 'I never thought I was a winner. It was great. Incredible. In those 10 or 15 minutes when I had to collect the Cup I would have done or said anything. That is how it gripped

SANSOM and daughter before a game at Highbury.

me. I couldn't wait to get up those stairs and get my hands on the trophy. I wasn't bothered about the medal, I wanted the Cup.

'As a kid I had watched on television as people like Emlyn Hughes lifted the Cup for Liverpool and his face always told the story of happiness. That is what I wanted. The lads said I couldn't wait to get up the stairs and they were right.

'Someone stuck an Arsenal hat on my head and I was later criticised for wearing it when I was handed the trophy. I hope no one was offended.

'It was the greatest and most exciting year of my life. I was a winner at last and that is the most important thing that has ever happened to me in a fantastic career. I also played some of the best football of my life until a stomach strain that turned out to be a hernia got me down.

'My wife, Elaine, also gave birth to our first son, Harry, born on Boxing Day and that just completed the story of that year. What more could I ask for?'

Sansom, overjoyed with his first winners' medal, left

Arsenal's celebrations that evening to attend the Professional Footballers' Association annual awards dinner where he was the unanimous choice as the First Division's finest left-back — the sixth year running he had won the award.

It is an astonishing record which fully emphasises the consistency and class he showed in his career.

But all good things have to come to an end — and the bombshell announcement on Wednesday, May 20, 1987 that Arsenal had signed a rapidly emerging young left-back from Wimbledon called Nigel Winterburn for £350,000 had Sansom reacting in typical forthright style with banner headlines expressing his disappointment and frustration on the back pages of all the morning's national newspapers.

He said: 'I honestly felt that we didn't need Winterburn at the club although I accept he is a fine player.'

But at a club like Arsenal and with a new,young thrusting manager in charge dedicated to restoring former glories, time waits for no man.

It was the beginning of the end for Sansom and despite another Littlewoods Cup Final in 1988 — this time defeat at the hands of Luton Town — Sansom eventually moved on to first Newcastle United then Queens Park Rangers.

The move North was precipitated by Sansom's blazing attack on Graham in a national newspaper about the lack of a new contract and the Arsenal boss was furious.

Yet watching Sansom wearing different colours when his teams visited Highbury made Arsenal supporters feel a little sad.

Kenny Sansom was truly one of Arsenal's most popular players — and a great one at that.

KENNY SANSOM'S PLAYING RECORD

	LEAGUE		F.A. CUP		F.L. CUP		EUROPE		TOTAL	
	App	Gls	App	Gls	App	Gls	App	Gls	App	Gls
1980-81	42	3	1		4				47	3
1981-82	42		1		5		4		52	
1982-83	40		8		8		2		58	
1983-84	40	1	1		4				45	1
1984-85	39	1	2		3				44	1
1985-86	42		5		7				54	
1986-87	35		4		9				48	
1987-88	34	1	4		8				46	1
	314	6	26		48		6		394	6

SCOTLAND: 1981 v Norway, Rumania, Switzerland, Spain, Rumania, Brazil, Wales, Scotland, Switzerland; 1982 v Northern Ireland, Wales, Holland, Scotland, Finland, France, Czechoslovakia, West Germany, Spain; 1983 v Denmark, West Germany, Greece, Luxembourg, Greece, Holland, Northern Ireland, Scotland; 1984 v Denmark, Holland, Luxembourg, France, Scotland, USSR, Brazil, Uruguay, Chile; 1985 v Egypt, Finland, Turkey, Northern Ireland, Eire, Rumania, Finland, Scotland, Italy, Mexico, West Germany, United States of America; 1986 v Rumania, Turkey, Northern Ireland, Egypt, Israel, USSR, Scotland, Mexico, Canada, Portugal, Morocco, Poland, Paraguay, Argentina; 1987 v Sweden, Northern Ireland (2), Yugoslavia, Spain, Turkey; 1988 v West Germany, Turkey, Yugoslavia, Holland, Scotland, Colombia, Switzerland, Eire, Holland, USSR. (77 caps).

CHAPTER 3

Charlie George

NO FOOTBALLER IN ARSENAL'S LONG, PROUD history has provoked such controversy as Charlie George.

Genius or headbanger? One thing is certain — we shall never know how great Charlie George could have been. And that remains the single biggest tragedy the game has ever witnessed.

For an all too brief spell, Charlie looked capable of becoming one of the best players British soccer has ever produced — yes, even on a par with someone like George Best. There can be no higher compliment.

Tall, slim, naturally graceful, Charlie could have the Highbury faithful eating out of his hand with one instinctive 40-yard pass placed on a sixpence or a thunderous volley that screamed past helpless goalkeepers.

How the fans adored him!

I know Charlie better than most — I grew up with him. We went to the same school in Islington, Holloway County. I stood alongside him on the Arsenal North Bank and even played in the same soccer team for a Sunday side called Mildmay in the Regent's Park Boys' League in North London. We've been pals all our lives.

In those distant days Charlie was always going to be the star. There was never any shadow of doubt that he would hit the big time with his beloved Arsenal. At 13 years old he could kick a ball almost the length of the pitch when the rest of us could barely manage 20 yards.

Now, when we bump into each other in Arsenal's East

CHARLIE — 'born is the King of Highbury.'

Stand — yes, we've both moved up from the terraces these days! — I can't help but think where it all went wrong for the leggy wayward genius who will forever hold a place in Arsenal's heart and history.

Not that Charlie is keen on any sob stories — far from it. Charlie did things his way and doesn't regret a minute of a career blessed with outstanding natural talent but littered with frequent bouts of depressing irresponsibility and controversy that blemished his marvellous skills.

I prefer to remember Charlie as the local hero from the Brecknock in Islington who made good — and who provided supporters with the kind of memories that will linger on forever.

And who can forget that brilliantly sunny day at Wembley on Saturday, May 8, 1971 when Arsenal, having clinched their first Football League Championship since 1953, with a glorious Ray Kennedy header at Spurs the previous Monday, were going in for the kill against Liverpool to complete an epic Double triumph.

ANOTHER scorcher hits the net — and look how the fans rejoice.

You can picture the scene now.

With just nine minutes of extra time remaining, Charlie picked up John Radford's pass, moved a few steps forward, and from around 25 yards hit a tremendous right-foot shot past Ray Clemence. Wembley went potty in a sea of yellow and blue Arsenal scarves.

It was pure *Boys' Own* material and as soon as the ball hit the back of the net Charlie — being Charlie — turned and fell on Wembley's hallowed turf with his arms in the air. Magic!

It was the crowning glory for Arsenal after an unforgettable season. As the whole of North London celebrated, Charlie said: 'As soon as I hit that shot I knew it was a goal. What a way to end such a fabulous week. First the League Championship at Spurs and now the Cup. I feel fantastic . . . marvellous. What a week! What a week! But I feel so tired. I could sleep for a week.'

CHARLIE lets fly down at The Dell — he was later to join Southampton after his Highbury career ended in disappointment.

And asked why he threw himself flat on his back he said: 'I don't know. That's me, I suppose, just me.'

Overnight Charlie George had become a national celebrity — to be fêted wherever he went, not least by the adoring Arsenal fans who loved him because he was one of their very own.

Naturally, it was a subject that Charlie loved to talk about.

He said: 'I'm an Arsenal fan. If I wasn't good enough to be out on the pitch, then I'd be up there on the North Bank.

'And I wouldn't be out of place. I know half the fans who stand up there anyway. I've never forgotten what a goal does for the North Bank. When I used to watch people like Joe Baker or David Herd we'd all go raving mad when they put one in. Just to show the players what we felt.

'These days I love to score at the North Bank so the fans can go mad for me. And I don't half show off for them,

THE unacceptable side of King Charlie — in fighting mood with Don Masson at QPR.

flinging myself on the floor or chasing round Highbury like a lunatic.

'I just want to get across to the fans how I feel. It's a great thing a goal. I want everyone to celebrate it.'

Charlie was only 20 when he hit his 'goal of a lifetime'

THE DOUBLE! Charlie and Ray Kennedy hold The Championship trophy as Frank McLintock parades the F.A. Cup after the greatest season in Arsenal's history.

against Liverpool and Arsenal fans drooled at the prospect of seeing him strut the Highbury stage for many years to come.

Indeed, coach Don Howe had even been tempted to liken Charlie's precious performances as a kid to those of the legendary Di Stefano of Real Madrid.

The next few seasons would, sadly, reveal a different story — public rows with manager Bertie Mee, the label of being 'lazy and inconsistent' and frequent misdemeanours on the pitch highlighted by a shameful two-fingered gesture to Derby County supporters after being baited at the Baseball Ground in a Cup tie.

Former Arsenal chairman Denis Hill-Wood — late father of the present incumbent at Arsenal — said at the time: 'If we transfer Charlie it will break his little heart.'

CHARLIE salutes the North Bank after scoring. They worshipped his every move.

ON England duty with Don Revie.

But Mee was gradually losing patience with moody, temperamental Charlie, and although he had been at Highbury since he was 13 the rift between the two became so deep that in 1975 the parting of the ways was the only sad inevitability.

The harsh reality of King Charlie's reign at Highbury is perhaps best reflected in his playing statistics — in seven years he played just 179 first-class games, scoring 49 goals after making his debut against Everton on the opening day of the 1969-70 season.

And with a talent like Charlie's up for grabs there was no shortage of bidders — notably from the club up the road, Spurs, where the George family had close connections. Cousin Horace Woodward was in the same Spurs side as the great Bill Nicholson who so brilliantly masterminded Spurs' Double triumph in 1961.

It was the shrewd, wily Nicholson who first cast envious

CHARLIE'S solitary England cap — against The Republic of Ireland in 1977.

eyes on George when the problems at Highbury started to multiply.

After Nicholson's departure from White Hart Lane, former Arsenal old boy Terry Neill took up the cudgel on Spurs' behalf — and even arranged a Press conference to announce his signing. But overnight Charlie was tempted by a counter offer from Dave Mackay to join champions Derby County for a paltry £90,000.

It was a move which prompted these words from Charlie's former Double colleague and now BBC TV presenter Bob Wilson:

'Charlie George is at a crossroads in his football life. Now he is ready to leave Arsenal, the club that have tried in vain to woo his unquestioned talents.

'George has long showed he has world-class potential.

'Not only should he be playing for England right now but also he should be acclaimed as one of the finest players in world soccer.

'He has the ability to rank with the Cruyffs and Mullers.

'But something has gone wrong with Charlie. I'm no longer certain that he wants to play. He has always had problems performing consistently.

'This has been the main reason for his failure to reach the heights he seemed headed for when he first stepped into the game.

'I remember all too well the first time I saw him. He was 13 and I was an amateur, new into League soccer from teaching.

'At the time I trained in the evenings with the school kids in their twice-weekly sessions. One of those kids was Charlie.

'He was class then. I've seen nothing to change that opinion in all the years since.

'Most players have an all-round talent with, perhaps, one or two better aspects to their play.

'Charlie was one of those rare players who had the lot. You can teach them nothing.

'I'm not exaggerating when I bracket Charlie with the likes of Jimmy Greaves, George Best, Denis Law, Johan Cruyff and Duncan Edwards.

'Yes, he is that good.

'But the sad part about all this is that Charlie has never been able to convince the footballing public that he is that talented.

'It is a tragedy indeed and it could be that the sorry tale will continue for some time yet.

'It will be strange to see Charlie leave Highbury.'

However, there were good times at the Baseball Ground — including four spectacular goals against mighty Real Madrid in a European Cup tie before Mackay got the boot and Derby went into decline.

Charlie eventually re-settled at Southampton under the guidance of former Guardsman Lawrie McMenemy. Down at The Dell, Charlie once again stamped his unquestionable class on the game.

It was at Derby that he won his only England cap against the Republic of Ireland at Wembley in 1977 under the managership of Don Revie.

Charlie was philosophical about the shameful manner in which he was internationally neglected and recalled the time when Revie picked him that once.

He said: 'Revie played me behind Stuart Pearson. Well, no disrespect to Stuart, but I don't think he was in the same class as me.

'Then at half-time Revie said he wanted me to play wide down the flanks. Me, a bleedin' winger.

'I thought to myself: 'Oh yeah. Thank you very much — and goodnight.' There is no bitterness. Mind you, if the gaffer had played me up front I think I'd still be in the team.'

There are those who remain convinced that Charlie would have been an even better player and fulfilled his potential had he started his career at another club — away from the worshipping fans who scrutinised his every move both on and off the field.

It is a view endorsed by Charlie himself.

He says, 'Not that I didn't love Highbury. Arsenal are a great club, and coming from that part of London I always wanted to play for them. But on reflection it would have been better for me if I'd started at a club like Southampton or, say, Birmingham, who really developed and looked after Trevor Francis. That would be my advice to any talented youngster.'

But try telling that to any of his supporters at Highbury where he is still held in awe.

No, they'd rather remember Charlie — warts and all — for what he achieved during his formative years rather than no Charlie at all.

CHARLIE GEORGE'S PLAYING RECORD

	LEAGUE		F.A. CUP		F.L. CUP		EUROPE		TOTAL	
	App	Gls	App	Gls	App	Gls	App	Gls	App	Gls
1969-70	28	6	1		2		8	4	39	10
1970-71	17	5	8	5			3		28	10
1971-72	23	7	8	3	2		5	1	38	11
1972-73	27	6	4	3	3	2			34	11
1973-74	28	5							28	5
1974-75	10	2	1		1				12	2
	133	31	22	11	8	2	16	5	179	49

CHAPTER 4

Frank McLintock

WHEN FRANK McLINTOCK GOT HOME FROM Wembley on the evening of the Football League Cup Final against Swindon Town on Saturday, March 15, 1968, the first to greet him was his five-year-old son, Neil.

'Daddy, daddy, where's the Cup?' he asked.

McLintock could have cried.

How DO you tell a five-year-old that the bottom had just dropped out of your world — that you had been to Wembley for the fourth time and still come home a loser?

That mighty Arsenal had just been humbled and then humiliated by a Third Division side to become the laughing stock of soccer?

That scene with Neil at the doorway of his home in Winchmore Hill, North London represents the lowest point of McLintock's career in soccer.

He was entitled to believe there was a jinx hanging over him.

Two F.A. Cup Finals for Leicester City, 0-2 v Spurs in 1961 and 1-3 v Manchester United in 1963 — plus defeat for Arsenal in the Football League Cup Final the previous season to the Swindon debacle — had given McLintock the title he loathed: SOCCER'S BIGGEST LOSER.

McLintock recalled: 'At 29, I thought my football life was over. At best I thought my only target would be to stay a First Division player for as long as I could, possibly another two seasons.

'I thought I'd never get success after Swindon. On the

McLINTOCK brushes up on his defensive partnership with Terry Mancini.

final whistle, I became so engrossed in my disappointment that I wandered aimlessly into the brass band.

'I was numb. Shot to pieces.'

McLintock joined Arsenal from Leicester City for £80,000 in 1964 — then a British record — as a tough, marauding, old-fashoned, attacking wing-half.

It was the season after the Swindon nightmare that coach Don Howe made the master switch which would lay the foundation stone of the modern Arsenal and provide McLintock with every honour in the game.

Peter Simpson, that most elegant of Arsenal defenders, had been hurt playing against Everton.

Howe, the coach who had marvelled at the play of Sheffield United's Joe Shaw — at 5ft 8ins the smallest centre-half in the First Division — switched McLintock to the No. 5 jersey.

'Frank wasn't too happy at first,' said Howe. 'He thought he was too short for the job, particularly winning balls in the air against tall strikers.

'But most time the big men only won the ball on the edge of the box and how many headers went in from there?

'Again I told Frank, like Joe Shaw, never to stand behind his man or side on when the ball was about to be crossed.

'His position was to be in front of the centre-forward, either getting to the ball first or either unsighting or unbalancing his opponent.

'Frank carried out the instructions perfectly. And because he has always been a wonderful competitor and distributor of the ball he developed at the age of 30 into one of the finest defenders in the game.'

And so McLintock, for the golden moments of his career, was content to let younger legs do the running while he conducted operations from the back and proved himself a shrewd centre-half.

From being one of the outstanding midfield men in the League he had disciplined himself to becoming the equal of the most effective defensive players in the game. McLintock was a commanding and inspirational captain who was respected by his team-mates for his great drive, never-say-die attitude and great tactical knowledge.

Above all, Howe's master switch was the very cornerstone upon which Arsenal were transformed into becoming one of the great sides of post-war soccer.

EAR we go! Frank in thoughtful mood during the epic Double season.

Like Alex James from the Thirties and Joe Mercer after the war, McLintock is now a legend in Highbury history.

In season 1969-70 Arsenal won through to their third major Final in three years — the European Fairs Cup Final against crack Belgian side Anderlecht.

The first leg took place in Brussels on April 22, 1970 in the Parc Astrid Stadium.

Anderlecht's star was Jan Mulder and he certainly lived up to his reputation — Arsenal were slaughtered in the first leg and were lucky not to have conceded more than three goals on the night.

Then, with minutes remaining, Bertie Mee introduced an 18-year-old substitute called Ray Kennedy and with his first touch made it 3-1 and, on the away goals count double ruling, there was a glimmer of hope.

Bob Wilson, McLintock's great friend, recalls in his book *You've Got To Be Crazy:*

'In the dressing-room Frank was hurling around some very juicy words to describe our performance. His strength was always his resilience and with Frank, despair turned into determination within minutes.

'By the time we were leaving the dressing room he was breathing fire — absolutely certain that we could turn the second leg around.

'There were 51,000 fans at Highbury on the evening of April 28. Not one fan left until they had enjoyed their fill of, perhaps, the greatest drama to which the old stadium had borne witness.

'Anderlecht far from settling for their lead came at us. Mulder hit my left-hand post with his first lightning strike.

'What we needed was the encouragement of a goal. After 25 minutes Eddie Kelly, another 18-year-old, got it. We were 1-0 up and 3-2 down on aggregate. In the second half, John Radford scored our second and at 3-3 on aggregate we were now ahead on the away goals ruling.

'Within another 90 seconds we had scored a third — Jon Sammels making it 3-0 on the night and 4-3 on aggregate.

'It's hard to describe the feeling at the final whistle. Arsenal were back in amongst the honours after a barren 17 years. After the gleaming silver trophy had been presented we began a lap of honour. It was impossible. Highbury had become a sea of bodies — with fans mingling with the players. The rest of the team turned back towards the dressing-room.

ON yer bike! Neighbours McLintock and George Graham joke around in the snow outside their Winchmore Hill homes.

The goalkeeper refused. I went on a solo run around the ground. I loved every second of it.'

For McLintock, above all the Arsenal players, the medal was the proof at last that he was a winner after so many Final disappointments.

On a night of high emotion the craggy little Scot from the Gorbals district of Glasgow blew his 'jinx' sky high.

It was just the start for McLintock as a rampant Arsenal suddenly found the confidence to go with their undeniable talents.

The following season Frank's immaculate leadership, commitment and style led Arsenal to the greatest season in the club's history reflected in this incredible week:

MONDAY, MAY 3: Crowned Champions of the Football League — won at of all places Tottenham, with a brilliant header from Ray Kennedy in the closing minutes after some 50,000 supporters had been locked outside White Hart Lane.

THURSDAY, MAY 6: Frank McLintock presented with the honour of Footballer of the Year awarded by the Football Writers' Association at London's Cafe Royal.

SATURDAY, MAY 8: Completion of the epic Double as Arsenal come from behind in extra-time to beat Bill Shankly's Liverpool 2-1 at Wembley.

It was the latter which provided McLintock with the outstanding memory of his career. A winner in his fifth Cup Final at Wembley.

And who would have begrudged him that distinction at long last?

I can still vividly picture him negotiating every Royal step on that triumphant ascent to collect the Cup from The Duke of Kent.

How sweet those moments — hugged and cuddled all the way up by adoring fans. Who cared about those exhausted legs that had inspired the Gunners to an incredible comeback?

Then the moment to savour — one he thought would always elude him — when he raised the F.A. Cup above his head to the deafening roar of the Arsenal supporters. There wasn't a dry eye in the place.

But McLintock, Arsenal to the core, is a proud and defiant man who justifiably took exception to critics who had slammed Arsenal's credentials.

ALWAYS super-fit, McLintock on the right track before a big game.

He said: 'We were a side that had no weaknesses — all right we didn't have the great players like the Bests, but we were 11 tremendous players. We'd fight and die for each other and, of course, that made us such a difficult team to beat.

'But if the Arsenal side that won the League and Cup was one of the most successful teams in English football — it was also the angriest.

'Angry because of the jibes we had to suffer. Angry because nobody, it seemed, believed in our ability. And angry because few people had any appreciation of what we were trying to do.

'I can't think of any other team in its class which has received as many jeers and votes of "no confidence" as the modern Arsenal.

'These remarks and many more like them had the effect of uniting our players in a common anger.

'There was a great pride in the team at Highbury, and the more our ability was queried the more our pride grew.

'I must admit that those remarks worried me at first, particularly the most common which was "no flair".

'Then I started to take a closer look at the Arsenal team — George Graham, Peter Simpson, Charlie George, George Armstrong. Well, if that lot had no flair there must have been something terribly wrong with all those attractive teams below us in the League.

'One fact which was of no help at all as we chased the Cup and League was the comparison constantly made between the Arsenal of 1971 and the Tottenham team which achieved that great Double a decade earlier.

'I suppose it's an inevitable comparison, but in my view, it's scarcely a fair one.

'You see, that Spurs team was a fantastic side — anyone who loves his football has to admit that.

'I used to go out of my way to watch them play and I played for Leicester against them in that 1961 Final when they achieved their Double.

'In terms of being attractive to watch, I don't really think the 1971 Arsenal team compares with them. But times have changed.

'It was far easier to play well then than it is these days; teams were prepared to allow you to play.

'Consequently, there were more contests of sheer skill, and nobody possessed as much of that commodity as the Super Spurs.

'I'd have loved to put the 1971 Gunners out against Spurs

McLINTOCK playing for QPR — Highbury fans could never get used to
him without the red of Arsenal.

in their prime. It's one of those enigmas that sports fans will
always argue about — would Louis have beaten Dempsey?
Would Ali have conquered Tunney? Would Arsenal 1971 have
contained Spurs 1961?

'I think we would. I think we'd have stopped them playing
their inspired attacking game and surprised them with the
power of our running.

'They, obviously, had more talented players in certain positions. Players who would have found places in any team. But they also had three or four ordinary players, weaknesses that we didn't have. I think our all-round strength would have seen us through.

'It'll never be proved, of course, but it would have been one hell of a match — and for a lot of people in North London it would always make one hell of an argument.

'They're great ones for tradition in that part of the capital we share with Spurs.

'I know my friends at White Hart Lane have often suffered from having names like Blanchflower and Mackay flung at them when things weren't going too well.

'And as a club which hadn't won a major trophy from our League victory in 1953 until the Fairs Cup in 1970, we were forever hearing about the glories of the past.

'It seemed, during the unsuccessful years, that a day couldn't pass without someone mentioning Chapman, James, Hapgood or one of the other gods.

'I'd never known a club so beset by tradition — and we were sick of it. Of course, things changed with success.

'The pressures on the players as the season reached its climax were tremendous. I felt this at its fiercest just before the Cup Final when, like the other lads, I was under all kinds of strain.

'A less understanding woman than my wife, Barbara, would, I think, have sent me packing rather than try to cope with my moods.

'I couldn't concentrate on the children, couldn't even put my mind to simple things like washing the car or cutting the lawn.

'The only time the pressure came off was when I was actually playing. That was a time when I could try and shape events instead of waiting for them to happen.

'There was the one relief during that last fantastic week when we had to beat or draw 0-0 with Spurs for the League and

TUNES of glory! Frank and his wife Barbara are piped in at a celebration
night for Arsenal's great Double season.

beat Liverpool for the Cup when I paused to collect the
Footballer of the Year award.

'But in the end the Arsenal side proved how well equipped
it was to succeed. We proved how good we were.'

The sweetest satisfaction for McLintock, I suspect, is that his side finally threw away the millstone that had hung around the necks of all Arsenal teams over the previous 20 years. The comparison with the ghosts of the past.

The talk in the pubs around Highbury was no longer of James, Bastin, Hulme and Hapgood.

Suddenly they were too busy raving about the depth of skill and character in the Arsenal side of the Seventies. McLintock added: 'The team realised an ambition I have cherished ever since I joined the club in 1964 — to play for an Arsenal side that was not living in the shadow of the past.'

How do you follow the Double? Getting to the F.A. Cup Final helped in 1972 — but defeat at the hands of Leeds (1-0) — meant that old hurting feeling returning to McLintock.

Yet he had the elation in January 1972 of receiving the MBE in the New Year's Honours List.

But in 1973 and with the apparent potential of a young Jeff Blockley emerging at Coventry, manager Bertie Mee hastily called time on a warrior he believed to be past his best.

If there is to be a criticism of Mee, it is in the hurried exit of McLintock in 1973 to London neighbours Queens Park Rangers — hardly a fitting end to one of soccer's great careers at Highbury.

The point was not lost on McLintock.

He said: 'You dream of bowing out in the way Manchester United's Bobby Charlton did at Chelsea — surrounded by sympathy and allowing yourself a bit of emotion.

'If it hadn't been for the silly statistic of my age, I would still be playing at Arsenal as if nothing had happened.

'I was as fit as ever. It was the thought of my age in the minds of the management that beat me. I'm sure that's all.

'I would have swallowed having to fight for my place, being in and out of the team, if I could have been sure of a Testimonial.'

Instead a man acknowledged as one of the truly great

inspirational captains in the history of football found a pay-off elsewhere — at Loftus Road.

It wasn't the way to treat a hero.

Arsenal, to their acute embarrassment, then saw McLintock's superb brand of leadership inspire QPR to the brink of the First Division title as the cracks at Highbury grew wider.

After two years at Loftus Road, Frank finally hung up his boots to try managership at his first club, Leicester. But less than a year later, disenchanted with the Filbert Street board, he upped and left before trying his luck at Brentford.

That, too, ended in disappointment until Frank re-emerged successfully with Millwall as No. 2 to John Docherty. Under their leadership the Docklands club won promotion to the First Division for the first time in the club's history in 1988. He has since left Millwall.

But the love of his life remains always the glorious Gunners he, more than anyone, helped fashion into one of soccer's great sides in 1971.

So much so that when his Double colleague and great friend George Graham got the coveted Arsenal job in 1986 he didn't bother to disguise his feelings.

He says: 'Yes, I was dead jealous when I knew George Graham had got it.

'But I wasn't at all surprised because George has done very well for himself in management and I believe he is just the man Arsenal need.

'Yet I couldn't help thinking it could easily have been me getting the call from Highbury if only things had gone a bit differently.

'Envious of George? Of course I am! It's a dream come true for him playing in the Arsenal side that won the Double and then returning 15 years later as manager.

'Once you've been an Arsenal player it's very hard to get it out of your system.

'I had nine smashing years at Arsenal but it didn't end well when they sold me to QPR. I always thought it would have been better if they'd kept me on the staff — the Liverpool way.'

Every Arsenal supporter would endorse that view.

FRANK McLINTOCK'S PLAYING RECORD

	LEAGUE		F.A. CUP		F.L. CUP		EUROPE		TOTAL	
	App	Gls	App	Gls	App	Gls	App	Gls	App	Gls
1964-65	25	2	2						27	2
1965-66	36	2	1						37	2
1966-67	40	9	3		2	2			45	11
1967-68	38	4	5		8	2			51	4
1968-69	37	1	4		7				48	1
1969-70	30				4		7		41	
1970-71	42	5	9		5		7	1	63	6
1971-72	37	3	9		4		5		55	3
1972-73	29		3	1	4				36	1
	314	26	36	1	34	4	19	1	403	32

SCOTLAND: 1965 v Northern Ireland; 1967 v USSR; 1970 v Northern Ireland; 1971 v Wales, Northern Ireland, England (6 caps).

CHAPTER 5

Jack Kelsey

WHEN WE WERE KIDS CHASING AUTOGRAPHS of our heroes outside the steps that lead to Arsenal's impressive entrance in Avenell Road, Jack Kelsey would first order us all to be quiet, insist on us lining up in an orderly queue, and only then would he agree to sign our books. Overawed in the presence of such a great man, we all stood to attention.

Other Arsenal stars were happy with dozens of kids simply thrusting pictures or autograph books under their noses in a general mayhem.

But Jack wasn't being difficult — it was a reflection of the disciplined way he ran his life and of the way he kept goal for Arsenal.

Simple, straightforward, no frills, no fuss — but as solid as a rock.

For 10 years Jack was a permanent fixture in Arsenal's goal — a tribute to his amazing consistency. Few people believe Arsenal have had a better goalkeeper than this Welsh-born tough guy whom many considered to be Britain's greatest in the Fifties.

George Graham, the present Arsenal manager, certainly has no doubts about Kelsey's claim to be Arsenal's No. 1 goalkeeper.

He says: 'Look back in Arsenal's history and the name Frank Moss immediately springs to mind. Frank was in the side that won trophies in the Thirties and for a decade was the mainstay of that great period for Arsenal. Then came George

Swindin who won medals as a player — and went on to become manager.

'Then Jack who had a fantastic career not just for Arsenal but Wales, too. He had such a love for this club — an Arsenal man through and through.

'In the late Sixties came Bob Wilson who, without doubt, was one of the best players in our Double year but didn't get the credit he deserved. Bob was very excitable and was a great trainer. We still laugh and tease him about the error in the 1971 Cup Final against Liverpool when his mistake allowed Steve Heighway to score for Liverpool.

'Who could leave out Pat Jennings? But Pat earned his reputation at Spurs. He came to Highbury when he was supposed to be finished but still had some tremendous seasons left in him for Arsenal. Yet I still believe his best days were at White Hart Lane.

'My Championship goalkeeper John Lukic must come into contention. I gave him his opportunity when I arrived here. I tightened up the defence and he proved one of the best shot stoppers in the country.

'Not having seen Moss, seen clips of Kelsey, played against Jennings, played with Bob Wilson and managed John Lukic I'd have to plump for Jack as Arsenal's greatest goalkeeper. I know the older fans thought the world of him.'

It speaks volumes for Kelsey's greatness that when injury finally brought an end to his distinguished career in 1962 many goalkeepers — Jack McClelland, Ian McKechnie, Tony Burns and Jim Furnell — tried but failed to replace him in goal.

Not until the emergence of Bob Wilson did Arsenal discover a goalkeeper of sufficient talent and quality to forget the name of Kelsey.

Yet big Jack's debut for Arsenal way back on February 24, 1951 had left Arsenal fans moaning and groaning — he let in five goals against Charlton.

In doing so he became the first Arsenal goalkeeper in 25 years to concede five goals at Highbury!

WHAT a save! Jack Kelsey flies through the air to save Arsenal.

But manager Tom Whittaker decided to give Kelsey another chance. Still Arsenal went down — 1-3 to Manchester United at Old Trafford! Kelsey was dropped.

Kelsey was born in Llansamlet near Swansea in South

Wales in 1929. His Cockney father, a smelter, was a soccer fanatic who helped run a local team called Winch Wen.

At five Jack was the club mascot and became star-struck at the antics in goal of Billo Staddon — and that made up his mind to be a goalkeeper just like his hero.

At 14, Jack went into the same Swansea tinplate works as his pals before trying his hand as a crane driver, then painter and decorator in his father's factory.

After National Service Kelsey found himself in goal for Winch Wen and after one particularly outstanding performance — he saved two penalties — was approached by two scouts asking him to choose between a trial at Arsenal or Bolton.

There was only one choice — and the young goalkeeper's breath was taken away by his first sight of Highbury.

Says Jack: 'It soared above the streets of little houses like a footballing Buckingham Palace. And the dressing rooms! There were baths, there were tiled floors, quite a change from the makeshift dressing-rooms in which I had been accustomed to strip.'

Strongly built, Jack weighed in at 12½ stone and stood 5ft 11ins tall. He soon regained the confidence of Whittaker who thrust him back into the limelight in season 1952-53 when, after the 11th game of the season, he made an unbroken run of 25 appearances to send Arsenal on their way to another League Championship triumph.

Tragically, Kelsey missed out on the last seven games when Whittaker decided to recall the experienced George Swindin to guide Arsenal through a nervous run-in to the title — which they eventually won, pipping Preston on goal average. Both Kelsey and Swindin picked up Championship medals.

But now there was no stopping Kelsey — Swindin played only two more games the following season before retiring and Kelsey made the first-team spot his own by right.

On March 22, 1954 Kelsey was selected to play for Wales for the first time — versus Northern Ireland at Wrexham where

WEIGHT for it! Kelsey shapes up before an important game.

he joined legendary team-mates such as Roy Paul, Ivor Allchurch and John Charles.

He kept his place and became No.1 choice for his country, winning a total of 41 caps.

A 2-1 win over England at Cardiff in 1955 was Wales' first victory over the English in a British Championship since 1938 and Kelsey's performance was simply magnificent, capped by what the newspapers described as a 'wonder save' from Don Revie.

But the real highlight came in the World Cup Finals in 1958 when, drawn alongside Sweden, Hungary and Mexico, Wales exceeded their wildest hopes by qualifying for the quarter-finals only to be paired against Brazil, who had introduced an 18-year-old scoring sensation called Pele.

Kelsey was an inspiration before Pele scored the only goal of the game 20 minutes before the end.

In his book *My Life And The Beautiful Game* Pele described the goal like this: 'I let the ball fall and then kicked it. To my disappointment I saw Kelsey dive to intercept, But just as he seemed to block the shot, the ball struck the foot of a defender and skidded past Kelsey into the net. Kelsey was a wonderful goalkeeper but we had won.'

Pele and Brazil went on to beat Sweden in the Final but the triumphant Welsh returned home to the Valleys with immense pride and with Kelsey acknowledged as the latest in a long line of outstanding British goalkeepers.

Then at the age of 33 and playing for his beloved Wales it all came to an end.

In the second of two friendlies with Brazil prior to the 1962 World Cup, Jack dived at the feet of Vava but the brilliant centre-forward's knee caught Kelsey in the back. Kelsey couldn't move a limb.

Back at Arsenal x-rays revealed a serious deformity of the spine which had it been discovered when he was a child, would have prevented Jack playing soccer.

He tried everything to make a comeback including having his torso in a wire cage for six weeks.

But there was no improvement. He could not raise his arms above shoulder level without pain. His great career was over.

Kelsey's international career with Wales brought him medals, caps, comradeship, trips all around the world and stardom.

AGONY for big Jack — injured at Wembley playing for his beloved Wales. Johnny Haynes is in the background.

Yet oddly he talked about the thing he would miss most — the loneliness of his job.

He said at the time: 'Many times in a match it is just you and the opponent. There is no cover, nothing between you and the net, nothing to prevent him scoring if he beats you.

'It is the challenge of this situation which makes goalkeeping so fascinating.

'It is just you, all on your own and him. From that moment the team depends entirely on you.

'All the other positions are interdependent while a goalkeeper relies almost entirely on himself.

'If he makes a mistake it's curtains. The loneliness is emphasised when play is at the other end because you are then merely a spectator unable to alter the course of the game.

'Goalkeepers are said to be the madmen of football. Well, a lot of strange things seemed to happen to me — broken bones, twisted knees, stubbed fingers.

'Take a game against Burnley in 1961. I came off the pitch feeling on top of the world. It was a cracking good game — we drew. And the fact that I'd dislocated a finger, damaged my ribs, strained my groin and knocked up my knee didn't spoil it in any way. I felt great!

'I've had my kidneys bashed, my ribs knocked in, my legs cracked and my hands battered.

'But it wouldn't do if you started thinking about injuries. You've got to be ready to jump head first at the big feet of some thundering centre-forward.

'You've got to do it without thinking and you've got to enjoy it. As soon as you find yourself wondering whether you'd get a boot in the teeth, you might as well give up the game.

'Crowds like the flashy goalkeeper — but he's not generally the best.

'To my mind the good goalkeeper is the one who always seems to be standing right in line with any shot that comes in, because he's the one with the positional sense.

'One of those rather showy tricks is to leap at a high ball and punch it away. Crowds seem to like that.

'Well, punching out a ball is something you should do only if a centre-forward like Bobby Smith or Nat Lofthouse is liable to shoulder you into the net holding the ball. It's an emergency measure only.

'At all times I try to catch the ball, bring it down, take a few seconds to size up everybody's position — and then do something useful when I push the ball upfield.

'I always carried a few sticks of chewing gum in my pockets when I was playing.

'As soon as I chewed a bit, I spat it on my hands and rubbed it over the palms. You've no idea what a grip it gives you on a slippery ball — even if it makes shaking hands a bit messy.

'Everybody always asks goalkeepers what was the best save they ever made. Mine was a save I tried to repeat for five years, because it so excited a man in the crowd that he sent me a cheque for £5.

JACK KELSEY — for 10 years a permanent fixture in Arsenal's goal.

'We were playing up at Newcastle, leading them 2-1 and then Bobby Mitchell came away with the ball on their lift wing — quickly. When he was about 30 yards out, he suddenly let fly with his left foot.

'Tell you the truth, I jumped more to make a show than anything else. I didn't think I could get to the ball.

'Just as it was heading for the top left corner I got my fingers to it and touched it round the post.

'Like most goalies, I used to find myself thinking I could do better than my team-mates.

'Well I've had my chances out in the field and I learned that it is a completely different world.

'Since I was little I've played in goal. When we used to go down the street to play, the other lads would be kicking the ball, but I would be bouncing it. I've always instinctively tried to catch a football, rather than kick it.

'Believe it or not, I am still as mad about football as I was when I got my first big chance at 16 with Winch Wen, a Swansea junior team and the only other club I've played for.'

After final confirmation that Kelsey's career was finished Arsenal offered him an administrative post at Highbury and arranged a bumper Testimonial against Glasgow Rangers on Monday, 20 May, 1963.

It was a magical night as 33,000 turned out to honour Kelsey, and with a then slim Jim Baxter turning on all his old tricks everybody — especially Kelsey with a £7,000 cheque to bank — went home happy.

In later years Kelsey could be seen running the Arsenal club shop, as poplular as ever with supporters and forever ready to swap stories of yesteryear.

He retired finally from Arsenal in December 1989 — after giving a lifetime service to his glorious Gunners.

He says: 'Football has been good to me. If I had my time all over again, I'd still want to be a goalkeeper — and play for Arsenal.

'The Gunners are the greatest club in the country.'

Last word goes to Bob Wilson, the man who has studied the art of goalkeeping and who comes up with this tribute to the great Jack Kelsey in his book *You've Got To Be Crazy*.

He says: 'Crosses, shots, interceptions, punches, kicks, throws — all were approached and performed with a tremendous air of confidence. Whatever fears may have been inside him, Jack never showed his worries. He could be spectacular but only when the situation demanded. His consistency became his greatest attribute.

'After the 1953 Championship medal at Arsenal, there had been no more domestic honours, just many unforgettable performances by him in goal.

'He had more than his fair share of injuries and in 12 seasons as a first-team player never completed all 42 games.

'Yet he always bounced back from the treatment table as bold, brave and brilliant as before.

'The older Arsenal fans love to chat to Jack recalling great games, great saves, and telling their sons and daughters about the exploits of the famous goalkeeper standing in front of them.

'Jack Kelsey finished his playing career just one season before I arrived at Highbury. His encouragement, advice and preparedness to listen to me provided invaluable help, especially in darker hours.

'Jack's career took him into the modern era, and yet his greatness stemmed from his early appearances opposite men like Sam Bartram, Ted Ditchburn, Bert Williams and Gil Merrick.

'His attitude, like theirs, was coloured by his love and loyalty to his club.'

Well said, Bob!

JACK KELSEY'S PLAYING RECORD

	LEAGUE		F.A. CUP		F.L. CUP		EUROPE		TOTAL	
	App	Gls	App	Gls	App	Gls	App	Gls	App	Gls
1950-51	4								4	
1951-52										
1952-53	25		4						29	
1953-54	39		2						41	
1954-55	38		2						40	
1955-56	32		4		1				36	
1956-57	30		3						33	
1957-58	38		1						39	
1958-59	27		5						32	
1959-60	22								22	
1960-61	37		1						38	
1961-62	35		2						37	
	327		24						351	

* Kelsey also played in 1 F.A. Charity Shield Final.

WALES: 1954 v Northern Ireland, Austria; 1955 v Scotland, Northern Ireland, Yugoslavia; 1956 v England, Northern Ireland, Scotland, Austria; 1957 v England, Northern Ireland, Scotland, Czechoslovakia (2), East Germany; 1958 v England, Scotland, Northern Ireland, Israel (2), Holland (2), Mexico, Sweden, Brazil; 1959 v England, Scotland; 1960 v England, Northern Ireland, Scotland; 1961 v England, Northern Ireland, Scotland, Holland, Spain (2); 1962 v England, Scotland, Northern Ireland, Brazil (2) (41 caps).

CHAPTER 6

George Armstrong

THERE ARE FEW FOOTBALLERS IN ARSENAL'S long history who have captured the hearts of the fans as much as George Armstrong.

In a club noted for loyal players, 1971 Double manager Bertie Mee describes George as 'one of the most outstanding club men that Arsenal ever had.'

Standing at just 5ft 7ins, Arsenal's little big man never knew when to give in — a player managers' need today to cure the insomnia and insecurity of their profession.

Determined and unselfish, he never shirked a challenge and combined his wing skills with a tireless enthusiasm that enabled him to chase and harry opponents into all kinds of error.

Armstrong's style was unique in many ways — he could follow any rigid tactical plan yet still retain the individualism and flair which earmarked him as one of the most dangerous wingers of his era.

Born in Hepburn, County Durham — hence his affectionate nickname Geordie — Armstrong first linked with Highbury back in 1961. Until David O'Leary broke the record in 1989, he held the distinction of most appearances for Arsenal — a mammoth 621 League and Cup games — and every one characterised by the sweat and honest-to-goodness effort he gave in their cause.

Goodness knows what sort of mileage he clocked up from his first appearance in Arsenal's colours way back on February 24, 1962 — a 1-0 victory over Blackpool — until he departed for Leicester in 1977.

My good friend and Press colleague Norman Giller once had the novel idea of charting his movement against Spurs from the first kick to the last. He wrote: 'There are 1,870 square yards of pitch at Highbury. George trod most of them against Spurs.

'It was exhausting to watch him move marathon distances at a sprinter's speed. He alternated between the left-wing, right-wing and a midfield defensive role.

'My clock-watching showed he spent 36 minutes in an attacking position on the left, 28 minutes on the right and 26 minutes in midfield defence. No wonder Arsenal claimed they could play a 4-3-4 formation with him in the side.

'Armstrong was in possession of the ball for "only" 92 seconds — 49 seconds in the first half and 43 in the second.

'But it was his industry and inventiveness off the ball that made him my man of the match.

'His positioning was dictated by the attacking movements of the opposition. If Spurs were raiding down the left he would switch to that side of the pitch. This meant his team-mates always knew where to find him with passes out of defence.

'Armstrong had the ball 38 times and made 30 passes, most of them short and quick and only six of them inaccurate. He was caught in possession five times.

'He took four free-kicks and 11 corners all with his right foot and it was his coolly delivered pass that made way for Peter Storey to score Arsenal's equaliser.

'Yet it was just another match for George. He ALWAYS runs himself to the edge of exhaustion without extracting or expecting praise for his performance.'

But Armstrong's efforts never went unnoticed by the fans who loved his all-action, all-out style. Admired by opponent and colleague alike, I cannot recall anybody having a bad word to say about him. Indeed there's a whole host of soccer greats queuing up to heap praise on the player labelled the 'Marathon Man' of Arsenal.

BOBBY CHARLTON (Manchester United): 'George was

GEORGE, pictured with his wife Marjorie, in his younger days at Highbury.

always a revelation playing for Arsenal. He always worked so hard — taking weight off defenders' shoulders by his willingness to get back and help out. I think he was as responsible as anyone for making Arsenal the success they were.'

MALCOLM ALLISON (former Manchester City manager): 'He had the ability to time and present the perfect cross. His elusiveness and most of all his sheer stamina was always a deciding factor for the Gunners.'

MARTIN PETERS (former Spurs skipper): 'George was one of those players who never got the headlines but deserved every recognition. He was a very accurate crosser of the ball and never stopped worrying when you were in possession. He did the work of TWO men for Arsenal.'

CHRIS LAWLER (former Liverpool full-back): 'He possessed this fantastic will-to-win and once he had the ball it was very difficult to make him part with it. He roamed all over the place and was so nimble.'

FRANK McLINTOCK: 'George was outstanding during our Double year. Yet the point is that he had been playing like that for many years but only then did people come around to realising his worth.

'George Armstrong was not just a footballer. He was a marathon runner, too. We had George up our sleeves for years. Nobody ever cottoned on to what a great asset he was to the team.

'George is the most unselfish, generous bloke I know. He hardly drinks but if ever he is standing in company at a bar he wants to buy all the rounds.

'That was the same give-everything attitude that came through in his game. He runs and runs and just when you thought he was going to collapse he'd start running again.

'It was the same in training. Most of us would be looking for an easy work-out. Where was George? Running, of course. But, apart from all the work he did, he happened to be the best chipper of a ball in the game. He could land it on a matchstick.

'George was one of those players who just got on with the job. You only started to miss him when he was out of the side. Above all, he was such a popular wee man with everybody — he always had a smile on his face.'

BOB McNAB: 'You could tell what we thought of George by the fact that in training six-a-sides he was always the first one picked.

'Then the trick was to let him go on a bit, then creep up and tell him he's having a bad game. He never argued . . . just

'SIGN here, please!' Bob McNab, pen in hand, gets plastered with George.

looked at you . . . then went tearing in like a terrier. There's no way he'd finish on the losing side.

'At the end of pre-season training we'd crawl off home to die for the afternoon — George would trot off to build a patio or plough a field or something!'

I once put the question of his incredible stamina to the man himself and he honestly and genuinely couldn't understand what all the fuss was about. 'It's something I never think about,' he said. 'Some players have marvellous skills and they can practically do anything with the ball. Others are really gritty and can tackle like demons.

'My game is built on running but I reckon there are other Arsenal players who do just as much as me. Perhaps it's my short legs that make me stand out.

'The secret of my game is to be a team member rather than an individualist. I never had a great deal of official recognition but I'm satisfied with the knowledge that I'm respected by players in the game.'

After his lung-bursting efforts for Arsenal, it is strange now to recall that Armstrong was twice on the verge of leaving Highbury and, on reflection, Bertie Mee was mighty thankful that nothing emerged from those unsettling periods.

A complete loss of form back in 1966 which resulted in him being dropped for a lengthy spell prompted Armstrong to slap in a transfer request. He said: 'I never really wanted to go but I wasn't achieving anything on the field and, being a little immature, asked for a move. It all blew up when I went storming in to see the then coach Dave Sexton to have a real barney. He just let me go on and on and when I'd said my piece he simply pointed out that I was kidding myself and the way I was playing I would get nowhere fast. I knew he was right.'

That wasn't the end of his troubles. Just three years later he became even more convinced that he had no future at the club when first Jimmy Robertson arrived in a swap deal which took David Jenkins to Spurs, then Bertie Mee splashed £100,000 on Hibernian winger Peter Marinello and he was slowly edged out of the first-team reckoning.

Then came the dramatic swing of events . . .

Armstrong came on as substitute during the first-leg clash with Ajax in the European Fairs Cup semi-finals with the score standing at 1-0 and immediately had a hand in two more goals to enable the Gunners to build up a commanding advantage.

He kept his place for the return in Amsterdam and was one of the stars of the night when Arsenal's superb defensive performance resisted all the pressure of the skilful Dutch team.

Armstrong left his most impressive display for the Final against Anderlecht at Highbury when his weaving runs and unceasing effort singled him out as the man of the match.

Arsenal, facing a 3-1 deficit from the first leg in Brussels, roared to a 3-0 triumph and gained their first major honour for 17 years.

It didn't stop there and no player worked harder than Armstrong in helping Arsenal land the coveted Double the following season. He was an ever-present in all matches and was named 'Player of the Year' by the Arsenal Supporters' Club.

Added George: 'When I look back that Fairs Cup success was a make-or-break tie for me. Luckily, anything I tried came off. It seemed my face didn't fit and I went out to prove them wrong. Since those dark days my life was never better.

'I've always said that to win a League Championship medal would be my one big ambition in football, but to get both honours in one season was too good to be true.

'After clinching the title at Spurs someone turned round and told us not to overdo the celebrations as we had another important match to play. "It's only the Cup Final," we all chorused and got back to sipping the champagne.

'Arsenal's leap to the top was a result of most of us growing up together . We'd been together since we were kids. I joined the club at the same time as Peter Storey and played in the youth side containing Peter Simpson, Jon Sammels and David Court.

'We were together so long that we knew each other inside out.

'Take youngsters like Charlie George, Eddie Kelly, Pat Rice, Ray Kennedy and Sammy Nelson. They had been at Highbury since leaving school. No wonder we possessed such a tremendous team spirit.'

He is quick to acknowledge the debt they owed coaches Dave Sexton and Don Howe. 'Dave was a master at making football seem simple and put a lot of enjoyment into our game. Don Howe made us into a great side. He organised the defence to act as our springboard to success and it just developed from there.

What rankled with the players was that Bertie Mee hardly received any credit for what he achieved at Arsenal. He had a tremendous record and his ability at picking the right men for the right job stood out a mile.'

'Geordie' is one of a family of nine children, seven boys and two girls. Like most local lads he had ambitions of joining

Newcastle United, and although he spent two weeks at St James's Park he was allowed to slip through their net.

He was only 17 when he climbed aboard the train to London in the summer of 1961 to accept an invitation from Arsenal scout Ernie Boak to have a trial.

Armstrong said: 'He had already got the three boys he wanted and took me to make up the numbers. It was holiday time and I decided to make the trip although I didn't think I had any chance of interesting Arsenal.

'I wore the No. 10 shirt in those days but manager George Swindin said he had plenty of inside-forwards and asked me to play on the wing.

'I wasn't bothered and my fitness stood me in good stead because it was a red hot day. I was invited back to Highbury and offered professional terms.

'I remember the first time I went to Arsenal's training ground at London Colney. I climbed in the van and there was this other lad sitting there. He said his name was Peter. Later, I heard his name was Storey. Us two were at Arsenal longest.'

Armstrong's progress was so swift that within the space of months he had secured a regular first-team place at 17.

He retains many warm memories of his start under Swindin.

'George was a terrific fellow who really looked after you. He was a real boss. If you turned up late for training he'd be waiting at the end of the corridor to give you a back-hander round the ear!

'But he was such a warm person. I remember after making my debut against Blackpool when we won 1-0 and I laid on the goal for Geoff Strong, he came running up to me and said: 'Bloody marvellous son.'

'As a youngster, those words meant the world to me. It was a very sad day for me when he left.'

In October 1974 Armstrong set a new appearance record for Arsenal when he played his 423rd League match in the big London clash with Spurs at White Hart Lane.

ARMSTRONG acknowledges the cheers before his Testimonial match against Ajax at Highbury.

He beat Bob John's old record of 421 League appearances set between 1922, when he was signed from Caerphilly, and 1937.

John won three Championship medals and three caps for Wales.

Despite a £20,000 Testimonial against Ajax in 1974, Armstrong had an unhappy end to his playing career at Highbury. He left Arsenal in 1977 after 16 years as a Gunner climaxed by a series of rows with manager Terry Neill.

A disappointing season at Leicester ended with a free

transfer to Stockport, then coaching appointments at Middlesbrough and Fulham before he quit Britain to pass on his skills and knowledge to top Kuwaiti side Al Salmiyeh in 1989.

George's life of luxury in the Gulf was a far cry from when he joined Arsenal in 1961.

'I got £15 a week then and even when I left Highbury in 1977 I was only getting £15,000 a year. A bit different from the lads these days!

'But Arsenal will always be my club — despite the last few sad months there. The fans and officials were always good to me.'

Armstrong's rift with Arsenal ended in July 1990 when George Graham brought him back from the desert and appointed him reserve coach.

It was a move which delighted everybody at Highbury, particularly his many fans who have never forgotten the little fellow's amazing stamina on the wing for Arsenal.

'Geordie' succeeded Stewart Houston, who moved up to fill the role of first-team coach after Theo Foley, assistant manager in Arsenal's championship season, had decided to return to his first love, Northampton Town, as manager.

No one was more aware than Graham of Armstrong's skills as a player and colleague in Arsenal's 1971 Double season. Graham realised that no player was more steeped in the traditions of Arsenal.

And passing on his vast experience to the youngsters at Highbury can only be a good thing for the club.

It's great to have you back, Geordie!

GEORGE ARMSTRONG'S PLAYING RECORD

	LEAGUE		F.A. CUP		F.L. CUP		EUROPE		TOTAL	
	App	Gls	App	Gls	App	Gls	App	Gls	App	Gls
1961-62	4	1							4	1
1962-63	16	2							16	2
1963-64	28	3	4	2			3		35	3
1964-65	40	4	2	1					42	5
1965-66	39	6	1						40	6
1966-67	40	7	4	1	3				47	8
1967-68	42	5	5		8				55	5
1968-69	29	5	2	1	6	2			37	8
1969-70	17	3	2		1		10		30	3
1970-71	42	7	9		5		8	1	64	7
1971-72	42	2	9	2	3		5	1	59	4
1972-73	30	2	7	1					37	3
1973-74	41		3		1				45	
1974-75	24		8	2	2				34	2
1975-76	29	4	1						30	4
1976-77	37	2	3		6	1			46	3
	500	53	60	10	35	3	26	2	621	64

CHAPTER 7

Joe Mercer

ON SATURDAY, DECEMBER 27, 1986 ARSENAL entertained Southampton in a League fixture at Highbury.

But it was no ordinary match.

For on that day almost exactly 100 years ago the legend of Arsenal Football Club was born.

From humble beginnings in those Woolwich munition factories in South London had grown one of the greatest soccer clubs in the world.

A massive crowd gathered on that cold, winter afternoon but the ground was soon warm with nostalgia and bursting with pride as the fans recalled exploits over 100 glorious years.

Arsenal had invited players past and not so past to attend the Centenary celebrations — from Ted Drake to Alf Kirchen; Laurie Scott to Reg Lewis; Joe Baker to John Radford; and Pat Rice to Malcolm Macdonald. Great players who illuminated almost every era of the club's history.

At half-time Arsenal's golden oldies were introduced one by one and cheered onto the pitch by delighted fans eagerly taking a journey back into time.

Then came the moment that brought the house down.

First came the famous 'grin'.

Then the famous 'cowboy legs'.

Joe Mercer had arrived!

Younger fans, enriched by stories of his greatness from their fathers stretched to catch a glimpse of a Gunner who is still held in awe in the marbled halls of Highbury.

ONE of the great managerial partnerships — Mercer and coach Malcolm Allison at Manchester City.

Older fans just felt very warm inside at seeing once again the man who, for eight glorious years, led Arsenal into the second great era of their history.

'Uncle Joe', 'Genial Joe', 'Dear Old Joe' — the memories came flooding back. A wonderful example of a man and a footballer.

Joe Mercer was born at Ellesmere Port, Cheshire on August 9, 1914. He joined Everton in 1931 and stayed with them until 1946 — playing 170 League games.

At Goodison Park he emerged as one of the greatest wing-halves of his time — winning a League Championship medal in 1939 in a team containing brilliant footballers such as Tommy Lawton, Alex Stevenson, Wally Boyes, Tommy Jones and Torry Gillick.

In 1938 Joe was the finest left-half in England. By the outbreak of war he had won five full England caps and he went on to win 22 wartime honours playing in a wonderful half-back line alongside Cliff Britton, his old Everton colleague, and

MERCER as England's caretaker manager discussing tactics with Trevor Brooking.

Stanley Cullis of Wolves who had been in the same Ellesmere Port school side.

He was the son of another Joe, captain of Nottingham Forest.

'I remember my father coming home from the First World War, when I was four years old,' he says. 'He opened his kit bag and tossed me a football. From that moment on all I wanted to do was become a professional footballer. But before Everton took me on I worked at Shellmex in Ellesmere Port, filling oil drums. I had to check on at 7.30 a.m. and my wage was 17s 6d a week. I turned pro for a fiver a week. It was a fortune. I used to count it four times before I got home.'

Mercer was still England's first choice in 1946 but after 15 years as an Everton player, his club and his international career seemed to be in decline at the comparatively early age of 31.

He was already actively concerned in a prosperous grocery business in Cheshire, owned by his father-in-law, and an early retirement seemed on the cards.

Eventually, Joe lost a little of his confidence. Everton dropped him from their League side and he asked for a move. The trouble was that his knee, injured in the 1946 England match against Scotland, refused to mend properly.

Tom Whittaker of Arsenal saw the knee one day when Everton were playing at Highbury. He thought he could do something with it — and if ever a man could it was Whittaker — and believed Mercer had at least two or three seasons left in first-class soccer. Everton did not.

He recalls: 'Everton considered I was a bad player. Arsenal told me I was a good one — under handicap. They restored my confidence.'

So Arsenal, second from bottom of the First Division, facing a £20,000 debt and on the hardest times the famous North London club had ever known since their formative years, snapped him up for a ridiculously bargain fee of £7,000.

It proved to be one of the greatest signings in Arsenal history.

From his very first game — a 2-2 draw with Bolton Wanderers on November 30, 1946 — Mercer's experience and leadership completely revitalised Arsenal.

Joe was a fighter, a shrewd tactician and put back club spirit and pride into a lacklustre side.

Joe weaved his magic — and Arsenal began to win games and climb the table.

It just went on from there.

With the signing of another craggy veteran Ronnie Rooke, whose days at London neighbours Fulham were said to be numbered, Arsenal suddenly and dramatically entered a new and totally unexpected era of success.

The Football League Championship was won in season 1947-48 with Mercer absent just twice and the formidable Rooke hitting the back of the net 33 times.

TWO cups for the price of one — Mercer with the F.A. Cup after City's triumph over Leicester in 1969.

Two years later Mercer led Arsenal to the F.A. Cup Final where two Reg Lewis goals put paid to Liverpool — the Gunners playing in the unaccustomed colours of old gold.

In season 1952-53 Arsenal were again acclaimed as League Champions — this time pipping Preston on goal average after a dramatic, nerve-tingling final match at Highbury against Burnley which they won 3-2.

Yet Mercer's influence on Arsenal was best illustrated in defeat — against Newcastle at Wembley in the 1952 Cup Final.

United were the Cup holders seeking to win the trophy in successive years for the first time since the late 19th century when Blackburn Rovers had achieved this rare feat.

Arsenal, who finished second in the First Division, lost ace full-back Wally Barnes after just 20 minutes with a badly twisted knee. No substitutes were allowed in those days.

It was then that Mercer showed his outstanding qualities of leadership. He magnificently marshalled his troops and Arsenal fought like demons to keep Newcastle out, but five minutes from time Newcastle's George Robledo snatched the only goal.

To Newcastle went the Cup but to Arsenal and Mercer went the glory.

At the post-match banquet Mercer, close to tears, said: 'I always thought the greatest honour in the game was to captain your country. I was wrong. It was to be captain of Arsenal today.'

Mercer also won the coveted Footballer of the Year trophy in 1950.

In 1953 Mercer told his adoring fans he had played his last match. Then he decided to play on.

But he broke his leg in a collision with Arsenal colleague Joe Wade in 1954 and his playing career was over.

From the 'scrapheap' at Everton, Mercer played nearly 300 League and Cup games for the Gunners, endearing himself to everyone with his insatiable appetite and infectious enthusiasm.

Mercer could not have done a better job in those eight wonderful years at Highbury — and his famous grin and bandy legs became a national institution in that post-war attendance boom.

With Arsenal he had altered his style of play — turning himself into a defensive wing-half, curtailing his natural attacking urges.

Denis Compton describes him like this: 'What a man! I played in front of Joe at Arsenal and learned to respect him as a player and person. You tried to respond because he was always setting such a fine example.'

Mercer stayed in football after hanging up his boots — first as manager of Sheffield United then Aston Villa.

HAPPY BIRTHDAY, JOE! Mercer takes the cake.

In 1965 he accepted an offer to take over Manchester City and picked Malcolm Allison as his right-hand man.

Together they restored City's pride and prestige. In five incredible years they won the Second Division title, the Football League Championship, the F.A. Cup, the Football League Cup, and the European Cup Winners' Cup.

Yet perhaps the greatest tribute to his managerial skills came when the Football Association — in between managers after sacking Sir Alf Ramsey — asked him to look after England's international side.

In seven matches during that summer of '74 he lost only one match — to Scotland at Hampden Park.

Mercer's most pleasing characteristic was that he never allowed the smile to be wiped off his face whatever the circumstances or adversity.

He says: 'Football has been my life. The game can and will survive without me but I can't do without football. I have so many wonderful memories and would like to go through it all again, particularly the springtime of my career with Everton . . . the wonderful Indian summer with Arsenal . . . and those hectic days as manager at Manchester City when we were winning everything there was to win.'

The humour is always quick to shine through.

One of my favourite stories that this great character tells is about the manager who, suddenly realising it was almost kick-off time, broke off a conversation with the words . . . 'Would you excuse me for a few minutes while I go and confuse my players?'

What makes it even better is that Joe tells it against himself.

He goes on: 'My spindly legs were first bared to an Everton dressing-room when I was a skinny youngster of 16. The legendary Dixie Dean took one look at them and announced: 'Son, they wouldn't last a postman a morning!'

'Later in life Dixie had a leg amputated and went to hospital for remedial treatment. The first time he looked into the ward he was confronted by patients with either a leg off or an arm off or some minus both limbs.

'Blimey,' said Dixie to the doctor, 'Has Tommy Smith of Liverpool been round here?'

Before the 1969 F.A. Cup Final against Leicester, Mercer challenged his City men: 'I dare you to go out and play football — enjoy yourselves.'

Once he gets started you can't stop him.

'I've always laughed — even after I had my slight stroke and nervous breakdown when I was in charge at Aston Villa.

'The doctor who examined me wanted his £20 fee immediately. 'Crikey, I must be a bad risk, doc.'

'You must have a laugh. There is no other chance of escape.'

'Apart from everything else, I've taken two teams down — Sheffield United and Villa.

MERCER the inspirational captain of Arsenal. He led the club into the second great era of their history.

'At Villa, we went down after Ronnie Allen hit an equaliser for West Bromwich which crawled over the line.

'In the office on Monday I was opening the mail when I noticed a letter postmarked Sheffield. It read: "Congratulations, you've done it again."

'I remember my first two games at United. I'd been given the job, my first as a manager, with the message by the chairman: "I know nothing about football, and that lot (there were 16 on the committee) know even less."

'Anyway we lost 4-0 to Newcastle and were lucky to get nought. We drew 1-1 at Charlton in our next outing and I heard one of the Sheffield officials comment: "The new man's not made much difference!"

'I'd moved to Bramall Lane after my career was finished by a broken right leg, playing for Arsenal against Liverpool.

'I was 39, I'd had eight years with Arsenal, and as they stretchered me off I waved to the crowd. It was simply an acceptance that I'd been playing on borrowed time, a signal of appreciation.

'There was even humour there. Most of the old trainers were groundsmen with a smattering knowledge of injury treatment. If hot and cold water didn't cure it they would say: "Oh, it's all in his mind."

'Billy Milne, our fellow, was a lovely bloke. But he was hard. If you were hurt, you'd get up quick for fear of him getting hold of you.

'Anyway, when my leg went they said you could hear the crack around the ground. It happened on the half-way line about 15 yards from the trainer's box.

'My thoughts went back to the story of a fellow who'd screamed when he broke a leg: "Don't let our trainer near me, get yours."

'The reply was: "But our bloke's worse than your fellow." I was shouting to Billy: 'It's broke, it's broke. Bring the ambulance".'

There's Joe Mercer for you. One thing's for sure — there'll never be another like him.

JOE MERCER'S PLAYING RECORD

	LEAGUE		F.A. CUP		F.L. CUP		EUROPE		TOTAL	
	App	Gls	App	Gls	App	Gls	App	Gls	App	Gls
1946-47	25		3						28	
1947-48	40		1						41	
1948-49	33		2						35	
1949-50	35		7						42	
1950-51	31		3						34	
1951-52	36		7						43	
1952-53	28	2	3						31	2
1953-54	19								19	
	247	2	26						273	2

* Mercer also played in 2 F.A. Charity Shield Finals.

CHAPTER 8

David O'Leary

EACH ARSENAL SUPPORTER WILL NO DOUBT have their own special memory of the night the Gunners became Champions at Anfield in 1989.

There is, of course — who could ever forget it! — the moment young Michael Thomas slipped the ball past the despairing Bruce Grobbelaar to clinch Arsenal's night of nights in extra time.

There's Alan Smith's marvellously timed run and header to put Arsenal on the road to glory from Nigel Winterburn's immaculate free kick.

There's the moment young Tony Adams held aloft the trophy to Arsenal's delirious travelling supporters.

There's the scene in the jubilant Arsenal dressing-room when a thousand flashbulbs popped as George Graham cuddled the glittering League Championship trophy.

And who can ever forget the performance of a lifetime from bargain-buy Kevin Richardson — so tireless in midfield?

Then there were the tears of David O'Leary — captured in millions of living rooms as TV homed in on a man whose emotions couldn't be contained a moment longer

An Arsenal reserve at 16, a first-team regular at 17, international star at 18 and, ultimately at 31, a winner of the prize he thought had eluded him.

O'Leary was entitled to cry his eyes out. There were not many Arsenal supporters who didn't cry with him that night.

For O'Leary it was the undeniable proof that loyalty is not the dirty word so many cynical people would have you believe

DAVID O'LEARY the family man — that Championship medal proves that nice guys don't have to finish second.

in football. And how Arsenal should be grateful for his dedication and service.

Back in the early Eighties O'Leary was part of one of the great teams in Highbury history — that fashioned by the managerial partnership of Terry Neill and Don Howe.

It contained the magical midfield skills of Liam 'Chippy' Brady and had the best centre-forward in the country in big, strong Frank Stapleton.

And the boy David, at that time, was regarded as arguably the best centre-half in Europe.

After a hat-trick of F.A. Cup Finals — Ipswich in 1978, Manchester United in 1979, West Ham in 1980 — plus the European Cup Winners' Cup Final in 1980 — the bottom dropped out of Highbury when first Brady was allowed to leave for Juventus in Italy and Stapleton went to Manchester United.

It was a bombshell from which Arsenal never recovered — and eventually cost both Neill and Howe their jobs.

It was only a matter of time, we all thought, before O'Leary would form part of a transfer hat-trick that would completely gut the club.

I believe, to this day, that had Arsenal held on to Brady and Stapleton the club could have dominated the Eighties with the sort of success to match the golden era of the Thirties.

But O'Leary, despite numerous big-money offers, wasn't tempted and contented himself that Arsenal remained the only club for him.

That's why those tears on that extra special night at Anfield were not just tears of victory, but tears from a man who knew he had made the right decision all those years before in sticking with the club that had become his life.

It's hard to believe now that O'Leary made his First Division debut against Burnley at Highbury way back on August 16, 1975. He partnered Terry Mancini in a 0-0 draw. He was barely 17.

Some 14 years later on November 4, 1989 he broke George Armstrong's appearance record of 621 games in the 4-3 victory over Norwich.

O'Leary remembers well that baptism of fire all those years before: 'I was soon feeling the elbows and knees of Ray Hankin and Mike Summerbee.

TALL, elegant and classy. The style of David O'Leary.

'After Summerbee had banged me over a few times he winked at me and said: "Don't worry son, you'll be all right".' How right you were Mike!

And soon the leggy, fresh-faced kid was winning superb reviews. The popular Mancini said at the time: 'This boy is one of the best prospects I've ever seen. He has a great future in front of him.

'He is so good that I know I'm only at Highbury while he's being groomed to take over.'

At 18, O'Leary made his international debut for the Republic of Ireland against France — yet it could so easily have been for England.

O'Leary was born in Stoke Newington, a terraced no-man's land that divides White Hart Lane and Highbury — and he lived there for two years before his carpenter father returned to Dublin.

England manager Don Revie spotted O'Leary at only 16 in a practice at Highbury but was told: 'You're too late, the lad has already played for Eire Youth.'

At school in Dublin O'Leary was denied soccer. It was all Gaelic football and hurling — 'Though I was too chicken for hurling,' he says. Instead, he took up running and football. 'He would rush home at night and straight out onto the street with his ball,' says his father Christie.

The big break came when Arsenal scout Gordon Clark spotted O'Leary in a Sunday League match.

Yet it should have been Old Trafford rather than Highbury where O'Leary would emerge as one of soccer's most prodigious talents.

When he was 13 he went to Manchester for a trial. O'Leary takes up the story: 'Shay Brennan had recommended me. They hummed and hawed and didn't seem to know whether they wanted me.

'Gordon Clark who was the Arsenal scout was just the opposite. Within minutes of seeing me play he said I would be a good player and I ought to sign for Arsenal.

INJURED and out of the action.

'I didn't know how he could tell me that after just five minutes but he must have seen something. Arsenal had just signed Jeff Blockley for £200,000 and it wasn't a good time for a centre-half to be going to the club — not that I thought about playing for the first team!

'Two other lads from Dublin, Frank Stapleton and Liam Brady, were at Arsenal, and though I didn't know them I was glad that a couple of players with the same background as me were at the club.

OH, BROTHER! O'Leary's Testimonial against Celtic in 1986 saw him playing against his brother, Pierse.

'Those were the main reasons I joined Arsenal — Mr Clark and the other lads. Everyone was so kind to me. Gordon became a great family friend.'

As O'Leary, Brady and Stapleton grew up together at Highbury, so one of Arsenal's great teams was beginning to unfold.

Yet it was the arrival of giant red-haired defender Willie Young from Spurs in 1977 that gave Arsenal the defensive platform for success.

The two couldn't have been more different. O'Leary was cool, calm and elegant. Big Willie was ungainly and crude.

Yet the pair of them had the time of their lives for four unforgettable seasons. Recalls O'Leary: 'When Willie joined us from Tottenham there weren't too many believers. In simple language I don't think our supporters considered him to be the best of buys.

'But he won the heart of the North Bank. We com-

THE tears of David O'Leary at Liverpool. Here, he's consoled by manager Graham.

plemented each other. I can honestly say I enjoyed just about every minute I played beside him. The only time we have had any sort of rows is when he tried to do the things he is not supposed to do.

'Let me explain. Willie was the best header of the ball in the club. He is a stopper. An old-fashioned centre-half if you like. When he stuck to that aspect of his game he was the No. 1 in the League.

'But every now and again he got carried away with it all. He started playing about with the ball — and that is when we rowed. He had to be reminded what his job is. Mind you, when he did wander it's only because he wanted to do well.

'I think when he first arrived at Highbury he was doubtful about his own future. But he has proved that even if he is awkward at times he was always positive.

'I keep thinking of all the great strikers he came face to face with in our time. How many of them had field days? Very, very few. Willie never knew when he was beaten.'

The pair starred in Cup Final after Cup Final but the departure of Brady and Stapleton soon had the club back in the wilderness.

As Arsenal struggled, O'Leary's form dipped and Young moved on to Nottingham Forest. From being hailed as one of Europe's classiest defenders O'Leary struggled to make any sort of impact at Highbury.

'I just don't know what went wrong with my game,' he admitted. His fortunes declined so dramatically that he found himself replaced as Arsenal captain and eventually axed from the Republic of Ireland team. 'It has been as much a mystery to me as it is to everyone else why my form suffered the way it did.'

Don Howe reckoned O'Leary's decline began when he lost the muscle-power of transferred partner Willie Young. Another theory is that he never quite adjusted to the shock of seeing his brilliant Irish compatriots Brady and Stapleton allowed to leave.

Said O'Leary: 'I suppose there's a grain of truth about the departure of Willie Young. We had played together for some time and had established a good understanding. That's essential for any central defensive partnership.

'But I don't think it could be put down to just Willie leaving. I think I suffered, like a few other players, because a very good team had been broken up and the club went completely off the boil.

'It was particularly hard for me because I had never known anything but glamour and success. I had four Cup Finals on the trot after coming into the side. Then came the worry of the captaincy. It just never suited my temperament. The captaincy should always go to somebody who really wants to do it. It's not something you can take on with any reluctance.

'I was relieved to hand it over to Graham Rix because it freed me of the responsibility.'

It wasn't until the arrival of George Graham — and a new

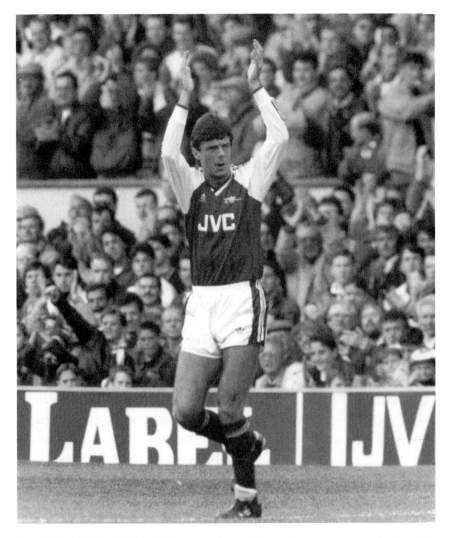

RECORD BREAKER! O'Leary acknowledges the applause as he breaks George Armstrong's appearance record of 621 games against Norwich at Highbury.

defensive pairing with outstanding defender Tony Adams — that O'Leary's career was able to take off again.

Graham, the hard taskmaster, says, 'I have to say that when I returned to the club David was a disappointment. In his younger days he was arguably one of the most outstanding central defenders in Europe, but for me he never fulfilled his potential. For a few seasons he was playing well below his best.

'I told him how I felt. I told him it was entirely up to him whether he carried on at Arsenal or not. David was out of the team for a while. But all credit to him, he came back strongly and impressed me. I know David well. I felt he needed geeing up and to be reminded that I don't suffer fools gladly. He responded magnificently.'

And if ever O'Leary needed an incentive to bump up his game, it was Graham's signing of Steve Bould at the start of the Championship season in 1988. Dropped, stuck in the reserves, O'Leary didn't get back into the side until Christmas — but once happily restored he never looked back.

Against Liverpool he never put a foot wrong against the combined might of Ian Rush, Peter Beardsley and John Barnes.

After the match, while his jubilant Arsenal colleagues were whooping it up with the fans, O'Leary was enjoying tearful embraces from dad Christie and brother Pierse.

The 31-year-old who had spent more than half his life at Highbury had bounced back from the brink of heartbreak to win his biggest prize in football.

He says: 'For the first time in 16 years I was contemplating quitting Arsenal. George Graham dropped me early in the season — and I was out for two months. I had never been dropped in my career and it hurt.

'I didn't think I deserved the axe — and I still beg to differ with the manager over that decision. It got to the stage where I was taking notice of the interest other clubs were showing in me.

'But I was brought back in December and I didn't look back. And winning at Liverpool is by far my proudest moment. That's why I couldn't stop crying.

'In fact, Liverpool goalkeeper Bruce Grobbelaar brought a box of Kleenex into our dressing room for me.'

O'Leary completed a night of personal glory by picking up the man of the match magnum of champagne.

He adds: 'I've now won the Littlewoods Cup, the F.A.

O'LEARY nips in to break down this Chelsea attack led by Colin Lee.

Cup and the League title with Arsenal and I've beaten George Armstrong's appearance record of 621 games.

'It makes my decision not to follow in the footsteps of Liam Brady and Frank Stapleton all the sweeter. I am proud to be a one-club man. Because Arsenal, for me, will always be the greatest.'

O'Leary is one of the game's genuine nice guys — and that League Championship medal proves once and for all that nice guys don't always have to finish second.

DAVID O'LEARY'S PLAYING RECORD

	LEAGUE		F.A. CUP		F.L. CUP		EUROPE		TOTAL	
	App	Gls	App	Gls	App	Gls	App	Gls	App	Gls
1975-76	27		1		2				30	
1976-77	33	2	3		4	1			40	3
1977-78	41	1	6	1	6				53	2
1978-79	37	2	11		1		5		54	2
1979-80	34	1	9		6		9		58	1
1980-81	24	1	1		2				27	1
1981-82	40	1	1		5		4		50	1
1982-83	36	1	5		7		2		50	1
1983-84	36		1		4				41	
1984-85	36		3		3				42	
1985-86	35		5		7				47	
1986-87	39		4		9				52	
1987-88	23		4		6	1			32	1
1988-89	26		2						28	
1989-90*	24	1	4		3				31	1
	491	10	60	1	65	2	20		636	13

* up to and including 10.03.90.

REPUBLIC OF IRELAND: 1977 v England, France (2), Spain, Bulgaria; 1978 v Bulgaria, Norway, Denmark; 1979 v England, Bulgaria, West Germany; 1980 v Wales, Bulgaria, Northern Ireland, England, Cyprus; 1981 v Holland, Czechoslovakia, Poland; 1982 v Holland, France; 1983 v Holland, Iceland, Spain; 1984 v Poland, Israel, China; 1985 v USSR, Norway, Denmark, Israel, England, Norway, Spain, Switzerland; 1986 v Switzerland, USSR, Denmark, Wales; 1989 v Spain, Malta, Hungary, West Germany, Northern Ireland, Malta (45 caps).

CHAPTER 9

Liam Brady

ON SATURDAY, OCTOBER 6, 1973 ARSENAL introduced a 17-year-old broth of a boy from Dublin to the soccer world in a League fixture against Birmingham City at Highbury.

Within five minutes of coming on as substitute for the injured Jeff Blockley, Liam 'Chippy' Brady had the 23,915 crowd eating out of his hand.

With a left foot that was made in heaven, Chippy — 'That's my nickname because I simply love chips' — launched the move which brought the game's only goal in the 32nd minute.

His magnificent crossfield ball found George Armstrong who helped it on to John Radford. His low centre was crashed into the roof of the net by Ray Kennedy.

It was the start of a love affair between Brady and the North Bank that ended in heartbreak in 1980 — when the most gifted Irishman to emerge since George Best, walked out on Arsenal at the end of his contract to find fame and fortune in Italy with the giants of Juventus.

They say that time is always a great healer — but Highbury was never the same place without Brady's cultured left peg sending defenders this way and that on his way to goal.

There is little doubt that Brady's game bordered on genius. His talent was so frightening that goodness knows how great Arsenal could have been had he stayed at Highbury.

As with David O'Leary, one of Don Revie's first telephone calls on becoming England manager was to Arsenal's Bertie Mee.

Revie wanted to know if the brilliant young midfield player qualified to play for England. 'Sorry, Don — the boy's Irish,' came Mee's reply.

Revie recalled: 'That was a tremendous disappointment to me. Brady's comprehensive range of talents stamped him as world class.

'With his excellent ball control, change of pace and confidence, Brady, like Johnny Giles and Alan Ball, was among the few players capable of dictating a match.

'Of all the youngsters I noted when becoming England's manager only a handful went on to improve their game. What particularly impressed me about Brady is that he rarely needed more than one touch to bring the ball under control. No matter how tightly marked, he always seemed to be able to create enough space to do what he wants. This is one of the hallmarks of a great footballer.'

How would you describe the genius of Brady? I'll leave that to the one and only Hughie McIlvaney, who captured the boy wonder perfectly in his column for *The Observer*. He wrote: 'Brady has a left foot delicate enough to pick a speck of dust from a baby's eye, a nearly infallible sense of orientation in the midfield along with the variety of passes to exploit it, and the confidence frequently to attempt and almost as frequently achieve the outrageous.

'On the field he appears as a slight, rather slouching figure but he stands a shade over 5 ft 8ins and weights 11st and since his heart is not readily discouraged he can compete where the fray is hottest.'

Brady first came to Highbury as a 13-year-old. 'I was playing inside-left for St Kevin's Boys in Dublin and a scout asked me to go over to London,' he recalled. 'I used to go to Arsenal in my school holidays and when I was 15 I signed as an apprentice.'

Athough his father had been a docker, three of Liam's brothers had played professional soccer — Frank for Shamrock Rovers, and Pat and Ray, who both had spells at Millwall and QPR.

LIAM 'Chippy' BRADY receives the PFA Player of the Year award in 1979.

Brady, alongside fellow Irishmen Frank Stapleton, David O'Leary, Pat Jennings, Pat Rice and Sammy Nelson, helped form one of the most attractive, entertaining sides in Arsenal history.

But despite his genuine love for the Gunners, Brady had a mature head on young shoulders. And with Kevin Keegan successfully lighting the path for British footballers to find untold riches abroad, the association with Arsenal was never going to reach maturity.

As early as 1978 he said: 'There is nothing I would like better than to stay here for the rest of my playing career, but for one consideration — financial security. The life of a

BRADY in a midfield tussle with Liverpool's Terry McDermott at Wembley.

professional footballer is so insecure. An injury can finish his career any time and the future becomes very short when you reach the early thirties.

'Because of the crippling tax regulations there is no way you can get security in this country, with Arsenal or any other club.

'It's like this — I know it is a horrible thing to have to say, but these days a man has to think about money.

'Nobody will want to know me when I'm a spent force in about 10 years' time. But I want to be able to show something from my career. That is why I will definitely go abroad when my contract runs out.

'I want to be a richer player, but I also want to be a better player.

'The point is I've got to go somewhere. Arsenal have been

THE long, lonely walk of a loser — shock defeat for Arsenal against Ipswich in 1978.

great to me. I wouldn't have a word said against them. They've offered me marvellous terms, maybe as good as you'd find anywhere. But they can't beat the tax system and I couldn't expect them to.

'Yet these days, for the first time, footballers can choose. They are not tied any more. They can actually go where the money is. And the way I see it, that means either Spain, Italy or Germany.

'It sounds kind of hard when you say it like that. I'm perfectly happy here. I'm with a fabulous club and lots of my friends are here. But I want to leave the game with something in the bank. In the short time I've been a player I've seen too many fellows dread the day when they have to pack it in.

'Arsenal are a great club run by people whose hearts are in the right place and, yes, I do feel a certain loyalty to them. But there's a greater loyalty to yourself.

'And, of course, I have always wanted to go as far as possible with my talent, to develop my game to the stage where

SMILES, this time — with his great pal Frank Stapleton after another match-winning display.

I can say: 'Well, I've done all I can with the ability I've been given.'

'I want to do what Kevin Keegan's done, which is going out and achieving something which people say is very difficult, maybe impossible. They said Keegan was mad to leave Liverpool. I thought it was a tremendously courageous decision. He went to stretch himself, build himself up to a new level.'

ANGER at Highbury as Brady lets his feelings be known.

In March 1979 Arsenal's most conspicuous and influential player of the era stood out again — when he became the first and only Gunner to win the prestigious Professional Footballers' Association Player of the Year Award at the glittering Hilton Hotel in London. He won by a big majority over runner-up Tony Currie of Leeds and third-place Osvaldo Ardiles of Spurs.

On receiving the trophy he said: 'To say I'm thrilled is an understatement. This is probably the greatest individual honour I will get.'

Then, with the characteristic Irish charm and twinkle in his eye that earmarked his time at Highbury, he added: 'I just wish Don Howe could see me sweating now!'

Chippy's' greatest glory for Arsenal came when he masterminded their first F.A. Cup win since 1971 — a 3-2 victory over Manchester United in the 1979 F.A. Cup Final.

He put the pride back in the Gunners with a sensational performance, destroying United with the sort of brilliant skills

BRADY puts his best foot forward with Arsenal physio Fred Street.

that the old stadium at Wembley hadn't seen since Stanley Matthews did his party piece in 1953.

It helped to make up for the massive disappointment he felt the previous year against Ipswich when red-hot favourites Arsenal went down 1-0 to the unfashionable Suffolk club.

And how the Brady bunch whooped it up — in the heart of rural Kent at eldest brother Ray's pub near Sevenoaks.

'It was,' Liam's mum Ellen recalls, 'a party to end them all! A candidate for the Guinness Book of Records very likely.' She went on: 'We finished about five in the morning. I couldn't

TWO of the game's biggest talents — Brady tangles with Trevor Francis.

help shouting when Liam helped to make Arsenal's winning goal scored by Alan Sunderland. My heart was beating so fast I couldn't think straight. Then Liam came out of the dressing-room and hugged me. "I did it for you, mammy," he said with his eyes full of tears. I cried buckets, only this time they were tears of happiness. The surroundings were so familiar that I couldn't help thinking back to last year when Arsenal lost against Ipswich.

'Liam sobbed in my arms then. It was a terrible time. "Forgive me, mammy, forgive me," he said. He was so ashamed. Even more of the family were over for that Final and he convinced himself that he had let us all down.

'While Liam was upsetting himself an Arsenal fan, a woman with her hair dyed red and white, would you believe, tried to console him by saying how brilliant he'd been all season.

'But those memories have been washed away now. Mind, I always knew Liam would win this time. Even when United scored those two late goals. Weeks ago when Liam was home I said to him: "I can't go through all that again. Are you going to win?" Liam looked straight at me and said: "Mammy, be there because I want you to see me with the Cup."

'Liam was just 13 when he flew to Arsenal for a trial. And he knew precisely what he wanted. Ever since I can remember, Bobby Charlton and George Best dominated his thoughts and I bet Manchester United are still kicking themselves they missed Liam.

'The plane tickets arrived too late. Arsenal scout Gordon Clark had been over and impressed my husband Eddie and I and sold the club to young Liam. United's ticket was on the mantelpiece when Liam left for Dublin airport.'

Brady's tears flowed again six months after the Cup Final When he was presented with the Player of the Year award by the Arsenal Supporters' Club — for a record third year.

Overcome with emotion as he received the award at the Empire Rooms, Tottenham Court Road, Brady sadly reaffirmed his decision to play in continental football when his contract expired.

Supporters' club secretary Barry Baker admitted: 'The fans used the occasion to make their feelings known to Liam. We had received so many letters pleading with us to get Liam to

CHIPPY'S greatest triumph — holding the 1979 F.A. Cup aloft to his adoring fans outside Islington Town Hall.

change his mind about going abroad. Liam was a lovely lad who always had time to talk to the fans.'

Brady captured 60% of the votes from the club's members to beat John Radford's double award.

However, there was disappointment to follow. Brady was desperate to leave Arsenal in the summer of 1981 with not just one trophy but two pots — but defeat by West Ham at Wembley followed four days later by losing the Cup Winners' Cup to Valencia in a penalty shoot-out ruined his dream.

It was then a matter of choosing the club of his future — after a career at Highbury that took in 307 first-class games and 59 goals. After approaches from clubs all round the world, Brady settled on Juventus — signing a three-year deal in July 1981 with a salary reported to be £3,000-a-week and a signing-on fee of £250,000.

Arsenal, under UEFA Freedom of Contract regulations,

received a maximum £600,000 as the transfer fee — a ridiculously low figure for a player of his stature on the world stage.

Brady is alleged to have had former American Secretary of State Henry Kissinger to thank for going to Juventus.

Kissinger, a soccer fanatic, was rumoured to have persuaded his friend Juventus boss Gianni Agnelli, to buy Brady in preference to West Germany's Horst Hrubesh.

Agnelli, owner of the giant Fiat car company, had set his eyes on the German after he had missed out on Kevin Keegan and Argentinian wonder boy Diego Maradona.

During a phone call in the middle of July, Kissinger is said to have told Agenelli that the German was rather slow and heavy in midfield and that from a technical point of view Brady would be a much wiser investment.

So Brady was no longer a Gunner and it must be stressed that, however hard it hurt them, Arsenal fans wished him luck as they waved him goodbye.

It is right to recall the parallel with Frank Stapleton who quit Arsenal at the end of the following season for Manchester United — a season in which Arsenal finished a creditable third in the First Division behind Aston Villa.

Losing two world-class stars so quickly devastated Arsenal. They never recovered from such a double blow and the Gunners entered a period of decline and depression. Yet Brady was forgiven by the fans because he took his wares to another country.

Stapleton, though, was needed at Highbury more than ever but came back to play against Arsenal. He received a torrent of abuse whenever he touched the ball for United at Highbury.

That didn't please Brady. Stapleton was his friend. He said: 'Arsenal suffered hard times after we left but the supporters shouldn't put that down to us. Other changes were made, too.

'The fans shouldn't have been bitter against Frank. He

MATCH of the DAY! Chippy on his wedding day.

went on to better himself and that was right. The real Arsenal fans will still appreciate him.'

Brady was an instant hit with Juventus — and how those fickle Italian fans worshipped him! He helped the Turin club win two League titles and became one of the country's favourite adopted sons.

But, with a year left of his contract, Juventus decided that Michel Platini, the gifted Frenchman, would better suit their team and Brady was sold to Sampdoria for £700,000. A further £1 million move to Inter Milan completed his education in Italy.

So Brady's voyage of discovery gave him everything he wanted — a world stage for unquestionable talents, wealth and a luxury lifestyle.

It was a far cry from the shy little lad who walked into Highbury, two months after the famous Double had been won in 1971 and endeared himself to everybody — chairman to tea lady — in ordering chips with every meal he ate!

Of all his great games and great triumphs for Arsenal, Juventus, Sampdoria, Inter Milan and the Republic of Ireland, I'll never forget Chippy on a cold, wet, muddy night at the County ground, Swindon, in 1979 in a Football League Cup fifth round replay.

It was one of those nights when it all went wrong for the multi-talented Arsenal side who found themselves 3-1 down with the home fans going wild.

Then Brady rolled up his sleeves and took control.

For me — and despite the F.A. Cup Final that followed that season — it was one of the greatest displays I've ever seen from anyone in an Arsenal shirt. Sensing that lesser mortals around him were off-colour, Brady silenced the home fans with a display of such authority that it was just inspiring to watch. He scored two goals to take the match to extra time and seemed everywhere pumping urgency into his disappointing colleagues.

Although Arsenal eventually went down to a dreadful mix-up in defence, the Swindon crowd that night were just as appreciative of Brady's giant performance as they were of their own giant-killing heroes.

The last word belongs to the great Johnny Giles, the man who groomed Brady to succeed him in the Republic of Ireland team: 'Every now and again a player emerges who is better than many of the great names of the past. Liam Brady is one such player.'

LIAM BRADY'S PLAYING RECORD

	LEAGUE		F.A. CUP		F.L. CUP		EUROPE		TOTAL	
	App	Gls	App	Gls	App	Gls	App	Gls	App	Gls
1973-74	13	1	1						14	1
1974-75	32	3	5		2	1			39	4
1975-76	42	5	1		1				44	5
1976-77	38	5	3		6				47	5
1977-78	39	9	6		7	4			52	13
1978-79	37	13	10	2	1		4	2	52	17
1979-80	34	7	9		6	5	9	2	58	14
	235	43	35	2	23	10	13	4	306	59

REPUBLIC OF IRELAND: 1975 v USSR, Turkey, Switzerland, USSR, Switzerland, West Germany; 1976 v Turkey, Norway, Poland; 1977 v England, Turkey, France (2), Spain, Bulgaria; 1978 v Bulgaria, Norway; 1979 v Northern Ireland, England, Denark, Bulgaria, West Germany; 1980 v Wales, Bulgaria, England, Cyprus (26 caps).

CHAPTER 10

James, Bastin, Drake and Hapgood

THE LATE, GREAT BOB WALL, ARSENAL secretary from Herbert Chapman right through to Bertie Mee, summed up the legend of wee Alex James with one significant story just after the European Fairs' Cup success against Anderlecht in 1970.

Arsenal under Mee and coach Don Howe had just won their first 'pot' for 17 barren years after a tremendous night of emotion at Highbury.

Wall recalled: 'The most vivid recollection of the club's Fairs Cup success had nothing to do with what happened on the field.

'The game was a great one but it is what happened in the boardroom after the Cup had been presented to Frank McLintock that made the victory complete.

'The incident came right out of the blue. One of the players — and I'm not going to say which one! — went up to our chairman Denis Hill-Wood and said: 'Now you know what you can do with your bloody Alex James!'

'A bit tactless, perhaps. It could even be described as rude. But for me it was like music in the ears. It proved quite conclusively that our present-day players had put the great Arsenal stars of the past in perspective.

'I know it has been said so often before but I honestly cannot overestimate the stifling effect our past success has had on our players. Too often they have been compared with the Alex Jameses.

'More than anything else that great win over Anderlecht set them free and it put the Arsenal name back on the competitive map. But more important still, it changed the attitude of the players.

'After all, how would ANY footballer feel being continually compared to someone like Alex James?'

Wee Alex was the greatest of all Arsenal players. Standing at only 5ft 5ins he was an impish bundle of fun, mischief, magic and mayhem to opposing defences.

He is one of only a handful of British footballers who bypass time — ranking alongside men such as Dixie Dean, Tommy Lawton, Steve Bloomer, Billy Meredith, Raich Carter, Peter Doherty, Stanley Matthews, Duncan Edwards, Bobby Charlton, Bobby Moore, Tom Finney, George Best, Denis Law and Jimmy Greaves in their contribution to the game.

The name of Alex James remains synonymous with Arsenal Football Club and the legend that was born back in those roaring Thirties.

And to gauge the extraordinary effect he had on Arsenal one only has to glance at the records.

This little big man from Kirkcaldy in Scotland joined Arsenal from Preston in 1929 — his name already immortalised in history after scoring two goals as a member of Scotland's famous 'Wembley Wizards' of 1928 who teased and tormented England in a 5-1 humiliation.

Before he arrived at Highbury, Arsenal hadn't won a thing — but in eight unforgettable, unbelievable years he inspired the club to four League titles in 1931, 1932, 1933, 1934 and three F.A. Cup Finals in 1930, 1932 and 1936.

It made Arsenal the team of the era and its very heartbeat was Alex James. For those eight years he, quite simply, ran the entire show.

George Allison, who succeeded Chapman, said of James: 'No one quite like him ever kicked ball. He had a most uncanny and wonderful control but because this was allied to a split-second thinking apparatus he simply left the opposition looking on his departing figure with amazement.'

Indeed, the most famous of Arsenal pictures — hanging splendidly in the marble halls of Highbury — shows a bemused Matt Busby, then a stylish wing-half with Manchester City, open-mouthed in awe alongside team-mates Sam Barkas and Jackie Bray as the wee man dances around them on the way to goal in a League game at Highbury in 1934.

Herbert Chapman used every trick in the book to land James when he was placed on the transfer list by Preston North End early in 1929.

The retirement of Charles Buchan had left Arsenal without a 'general' on the field and Chapman realised immediately that Alex was the man to light the fire at Highbury.

The only obstacles he faced were Liverpool, Manchester City and Aston Villa — and Alex James himself!

James, a dapper little man and extrovert extraordinary — he frequently wore loud, garish, tartan checks, spats and bow-ties — wasn't slow in estimating his own worth as a footballer. He knew he was the best and was determined to get the most out of his transfer.

In John Harding's brilliant biography entitled *Alex James: Life of a Football Legend*, James wrote: 'The only time a footballer can call his name and ability his own is when it comes to that little matter of dipping pen in the ink and writing a signature across the form.'

Joining clubs with great pasts, great potential, and great players meant nothing to him. He was concerned with one thing. 'Dear old Jock Ewert, my playing pal at Preston, used to tell me: 'Get all you can out of this racket. You're worth it. People who come to watch Preston only come to see you. Cash in while you can.'

'Prominent players just then were being offered business opportunities in the larger towns. I was coming in for a good

ALEX JAMES, a dapper little man and an extrovert extraordinary. Before he arrived at Highbury Arsenal hadn't won a thing. But in eight unforgettable years after his transfer from Preston he inspired the Gunners to four League titles and three F.A. Cup Finals.

deal of favourable notice, so why should my thoughts not turn to business, too?'

What, in effect, he was hinting at was that he wanted a considerable amount of cash as an under-the-counter payment — a direct breach of Football League rules! So after he had turned down Liverpool, City and then Villa, soccer's top brass were beginning to get suspicious when Chapman made his move in May, 1929.

The astute Yorkshireman, however, was not one to be beaten — announcing a scheme to solve 'Alex's difficulties'.

A job had been arranged for him outside football.

'You will act as a sports demonstrator at Selfridges, a West End store, at a salary of £250 a year. I have arranged a two-year contract for you,' said Chapman.

There were no rules to prevent a professional footballer having two jobs, so the Football League were stumped.

They held an inquiry — but Arsenal and Chapman had got their man! James continued: 'It was just what I wanted. I was given details of the work and accepted at once. All along I felt that London was the best place in which I could land.

'Mr A. H. Williams was my boss at Selfridges and he started pointing out to me the value of publicity even to a footballer. He showed me how headlines, pictures and cartoons would put me on the map as much as my football skills.

'My long shorts were already known. Folks would say: 'That's Alex James, the little fellow in the long knickers.' Publicity for a footballer! But it worked.

'The store plastered my name and face all over the newspapers and people came into Selfridges in their hundreds to see the £9,000 new man of Arsenal. I was being built up into something more than a footballer. I was becoming a crowd puller already.'

However, there were drawbacks. He added: 'My job kept me in the West End in the evenings and I found too many people anxious to show me London by night when I had finished at the store. I fell into parties and found myself at all kinds of queer dives and nightclubs at an hour when any footballer ought to be fast asleep. The lights and the flash company went to my head in those early days, or rather nights!'

James's trademark, of course, were those long baggy

JAMES in his early days at Arsenal. He was to become the greatest Gunner of them all.

shorts and they became a household talking point. But they were not his idea.

That novel invention belonged to *Daily Mail* cartoonist Tom Webster who drew him in long knickers one Monday morning after a game for Preston to emphasise James's diminutive stature. Alex loved the idea! Ever ready to cash in on any publicity gimmick, he then insisted on wearing long baggy shorts — tailor-made, of course — for the rest of his incredible career. His excuse was that it kept his knees warm!

Chapman, ever careful not to upset the man he knew would pilot Arsenal to glory, always treated him differently from the other Arsenal players.

James was allowed to stay in bed until noon on match days, for example.

That was until James refused to re-sign in the summer of 1931 — when he was looking for extra inducements. So Chapman sent him on a holiday — a cruise.

James, however, realised that you don't cross Chapman too often. He discovered that his 'cruise' was on a banana and general cargo boat and he had to work his passage.

Released in Bordeaux, James had got the message and promptly signed on again to resume his feats for Arsenal.

James was originally a goalscoring inside-forward but Chapman converted him into being the arch schemer — the man who conducted the orchestra.

Without him, many critics believe the style, the system and successes would never have been achieved.

It is strange now to recall that James had a disappointing start at Highbury — finding it difficult to settle down.

The turning point for James and Arsenal came on the evening of Saturday, January 25, 1930 after a lucky F.A. Cup Fourth Round 2-2 draw with Birmingham at Highbury.

That night Chapman made the decision that changed the history of Arsenal Football Club.

He visited Alex James who had been dropped and sent home after the Gunners had won just five of the previous 20 games. Chapman, using every ounce of theatre, told James that Arsenal's whole season — and probably their futures — relied totally on his performance in the replay at St Andrew's that Wednesday.

JAMES, in his famous baggy shorts, has a fitness test before a big game.

Chapman's battlecry was just the tonic James's bruised ego needed. He responded instantly and starred in a magnificent 1-0 victory that eventually led to the club's first major honour — the 2-0 F.A. Cup Final victory over Huddersfield at Wembley Stadium on April 26, 1930.

Arsenal, Chapman and James would never look back.

In all, he made 261 appearances for Arsenal (26 goals) and was captain for five years. He was captain of Arsenal in 1936 when Ted Drake's solitary goal against Sheffield United took the Cup back to North London.

James retired in 1937 but returned to Arsenal after the war to coach the 'A' side at Hendon.

A man who lived life to the full, he died from cancer in June 1953 but his greatness is such that he'll be remembered whenever the name of Arsenal is mentioned.

CLIFF 'BOY' BASTIN joined Arsenal two weeks after James and, as personalities, they were as different as chalk and cheese.

Yet, together they formed the greatest wing partnership in the history of football let alone Arsenal.

Within days of Bastin arriving at the club, James predicted: 'This boy Bastin will be one of the greatest forwards soccer has ever known.' How right he was.

Tom Whittaker said of Bastin: 'Coupled with his sincerity and his loyalty to all his bosses he had a trait few of us are blessed with, that is, he had an ice-cold temperament.'

This was never better illustrated than when Bastin signed for Arsenal. At only 17 he was working in a pump yard of a farm in his native Devon when his boss, an electrical engineer, asked: 'How would you like to play for the famous Arsenal?'

Bastin and his boss discussed the move further on the short drive to Exeter.

They then met with Herbert Chapman in the offices of Dunn & Baker, Solicitors. The move was discussed even further around the dining table of the Bastin family home in Exeter.

Finally, to Chapman's great relief, Bastin signed for a fee of £2,000.

He then promptly thanked the flabbergasted Arsenal manager and went off to play tennis at a local club!

CLIFF 'Boy' BASTIN showing the style that made him one of soccer's all-time greats.

All this for a boy discovered quite by accident.

Chapman, accompanied by George Allison, had travelled to Vicarage Road, Watford to look at a local player. But another footballer immediately caught his eye — playing for their opponents, Exeter City.

The programme picked him out as 'C. Bastin' — a fair-haired, stockily build lad playing at inside-left. He was only 16.

Bastin amazed them with his ball control, coolness and confidence. His positional sense was uncanny. He collected the ball and used it with the judgement of a player twice his age.

Chapman knew instantly he was looking at a player who would one day rank with soccer's immortals. He remarked to Allison: 'Arsenal must have this boy.'

What happened once Bastin arrived at Highbury is pure fairytale material — winning all the game's biggest honours before he was 21. He won an F.A. Cup Winners medal at 18, a League Championship medal at 19 and an England cap at 20.

In 1933 Bastin set up a Football League record by scoring 33 goals from his left-wing berth. It is a record that still stands today.

When no one else could guess Alex James' next move, Bastin always knew what to expect. The partnership was uncanny and devastated defences the length and breadth of the country.

Bastin never gave up the view that he was a better inside-forward — although he was happy to play in any position Herbert Chapman picked for him. England's selectors often agreed. In 13 of his 21 games for England Bastin played at inside-forward and partnered Eric Brook, the unorthodox Manchester City winger.

Like Bastin, Brook never believed in hugging the touchlines and their top-speed switches totally confused England's opponents.

Bastin's first match for Arsenal was against Everton at Goodison Park on October 5, 1929. He went on to play 395 games in the famous red and white Arsenal jersey and scored 178 goals. In 21 England internationals he hit the back of the net 12 times.

The great Charles Buchan paid Bastin this handsome

BASTIN joined Arsenal at 17 and went out to play 395 games for Arsenal.

tribute: 'Bastin had neither the artistry of a Stanley Matthews nor the speed of a sprinter, but I think he was the most effective wing-forward I ever saw during my long experience.

'Bastin had an uncanny knack of sizing up the situation in a split second and the timing necessary to make the best use of it. As a positional player in front of goal he had no superior.

'Ever ready to take advantage of an opening, Cliff had a deadly shot in either foot. He holds the League scoring record for a wing-forward. Arsenal owed much to an ice-cool brain that enabled Cliff to turn to advantage the slightest mistake made by the opposition.

'Blessed with a wonderful physique, Bastin took all the knocks with exemplary fortitude. I never saw him do a mean action on the field. He was a club man all the time. Arsenal have had no more valuable player on their books.'

On Boxing Day, 1946 — after 17 years at Highbury — he played his last game for Arsenal, captaining the reserve side against Cardiff City.

It was disclosed then that Bastin had been deaf for nearly 10 years and that it was necessary for him to have a major operation to restore his middle ear.

He retired to his native Exeter and became a publican in the village of Heavietree.

His fondest memory: 'I was just 17, and scored the equalising goal against Hull City in the last two minutes of the F.A. Cup semi-final at Leeds.

'We won the replay at Villa Park and then beat Huddersfield at Wembley to land Arsenal's first-ever honour. At 17 I felt on top of the world.'

Bastin was a quiet and gentle man on and off the field until in retirement he made a stinging attack on modern footballers. In an interview with Brian Scovell of the *Daily Mail* in 1969 he said: 'When I read about a bruised toe keeping a player out I have a chuckle. One Christmas I stuck my foot in a scalding hot slipper bath by mistake and the whole foot came up in a huge blister. Tom Whittaker, then the Arsenal trainer, told me he could strap up my foot if I wanted to play. He strapped the foot up and I played. During the game the blister burst, but I played on until the end.

'Mind you, we used to take a lot of care protecting ourselves. I used to put cotton wool under my shinguards. They were big, heavy shinguards. Not the ones they have now. Some players don't even use shinguards today. They're asking for trouble.

'The boots we had — the old Hotspur was one I remember — used to come right above the ankle so you got extra protection that way. The toecap was solid leather with a small

TWO of soccer's legends pictured at Highbury — Bastin moves in to block this cross from Derby's Raich Carter.

steel tip to it. If you got kicked with one of those you felt it! I wouldn't have been able to last the pace with today's footwear, I'd be out half the season.

'One player who rose to a high position in the Players' Union used to say to me: 'I'll break your leg.' But Wilf Copping used to take care of me. He'd sort them out!

'The game is not so tough as it used to be. The tackling is not so hard. There's more petty things happening today.

'English teams are playing like the Continentals used to — pattern-weaving and a lot of passing. Pretty to watch, but I preferred the old style — wingers going up the wing and long passes.'

His greatness is perhaps best described by leading journalist of the Thirties Frank M. Carruthers who wrote the following after a stunning Bastin perfomance in an inter-league England v Ireland match at Preston in 1933.

'I cannot recall any English footballer who ever enjoyed a greater triumph than Bastin. He was acclaimed by everyone a genius, the supreme master of forward play.

'He dominated the match, and the public rose to him. He played the ball five times to any other man's once, and it was perhaps this more than anything else which revealed his greatness. He found the open spaces which are ever the haunt of the craftsman, making it so easy for his colleagues to give him the ball. His sense of anticipation and positional play was truly wonderful.

'Success has not spoilt Bastin. He has won every honour that can go to the footballer and yet he is as shy and as modest as when he first joined the Arsenal side.

'After the match at Preston he was chased by a hundred or more autograph hunters and pleaded for someone to get him away. Finally he made a dash for a motor-car and he was not happy until he had hidden himself in a corner of the train. "I hate all this fuss," he told me.'

TED DRAKE will always be remembered for the seven goals he scored for Arsenal against Aston Villa at Villa Park on December 14, 1935.

Southampton-born, he was George Allison's first signing for Arsenal. Standing at 5ft 10ins and weighing 12st 10lbs, he is the most famous of all Arsenal centre-forwards — and one of soccer's all-time greats.

Drake, rugged, muscular and recklessly brave, scored four goals in a match four times and grabbed three goals in England's 6-2 win over Hungary in December 1936.

His goal tally in six seasons for Arsenal was 123 in 168 First Division appearances plus 12 goals from 14 Cup matches.

He also hit six goals in five games for England. His philosophy is a simple one: 'Centre-forwards must give and take. But if I had my time all over again I would never play anywhere else. It is unquestionably the most glamorous position to play in but it can be equally frustrating.

TED DRAKE in retirement holding the ball that hit the Villa net a record seven times.

'Certain qualities are necessary to be a centre-forward — ability, height, pace, a good head and two good feet and, above all, bravery.'

Drake used the lot at Villa Park in the most incredible individual goalscoring feat in football. He recalled: 'I remember it was touch and go whether I turned out at Villa Park because I'd been injured playing for England against Wales.

WITH Bobby Moore and Alan Mullery at Fulham where Drake became Chief Scout.

'I'd never gone on the field strapped up before. They put this heavy bandage on my wonky left knee but I soon forgot about it as the goals went in.

'Villa were so good about it afterwards. They signed the ball and presented it to me. I've still got it. Do you know it's the only souvenir I have left in my career — all my caps and medals were stolen when my house was burgled some years ago.

What makes Drake's scoring feat so incredible was that he actually scored seven goals from EIGHT shots! The other one hit the bar!

'People still can't believe it,' he added. 'Why, sometimes, you don't see eight shots in one match from all the players out together. Oddly enough, it's the one that got away that sticks with me.

'I hit the underside of the bar, the ball dropped down over

WEDDING DAY joy for Ted and Mrs Ted Drake.

the line and out. The referee waved aside my appeals and said: 'Don't be greedy. Isn't seven enough?'

'That's the way we played it then. Bit of fun. Bit of fire. And we were Arsenal. Mustn't argue. Tradition, you know. What a marvellous club!

'What set me off was an accident. We were warming up and I went to collect the ball on the running track. But my studs stuck in the mud and I fell over, grazing my arm. The fans loved it, jeering and laughing. I got up, rubbed off the cinders and thought: "You'll pay for that!" They did as well.

'But we didn't celebrate. Our only thought was getting the 5.30 train from Snow Hill station back to London.'

Drake's goals are the stuff of which legends are made.

Bernard Joy recalled: 'It was the fearsome accuracy of Ted Drake's shooting rather than his records which made him so memorable.

'He attributes the accuracy to advice from Alex James. Drake explained to me: "During shooting practice Alex told me never to stop the ball because there is no time to do so in a match. I had to hit it on the drop, on the turn, on the volley — however it came. I kept my eye on the ball, ignoring what went on around, because once you lift your head you lose accuracy."

'Playing behind Ted as I used to, it was stimulating to see the broad shoulder cleave a vivid red path through the middle.

'He had pace, power and resolution and the first two goals against Villa came after beating the centre-half and racing the backs as they closed in.

'He scored a hat-trick in the first half, notched another within 13 minutes of the restart and reached the record in the last minute from a centre by Cliff Bastin.

'Drake joined Arsenal from Southampton in March 1934 for £6,000 and in his first full season he scored 42 goals — still a club record.

'He topped Arsenal's scorers in the five seasons before the war, helping the club to two League titles and an F.A. Cup triumph.

'When playing for Preston against Arsenal, Bill Shankly saw Drake hit an unforgettable goal. He recalled: "Dear God, that shot was frightening. If our goalkeeper had got his hands to it, it would have taken them off."

'Drake's fearless, go-for-goal style inevitably brought injuries and he was limited to five England internationals in which he scored six goals.'

Drake made his England debut in the infamous 'Battle of Highbury' — against World Champions Italy in November, 1934.

Italian dictator Benito Mussolini had ordered an urgent

TED DRAKE pictured with Frank Blunstone, Peter Brabrook and Jimmy Greaves in his days as Chelsea boss.

telegram to be despatched to his countrymen before the match. It read: 'FOR YOUR COUNTRY'S SAKE . . . WIN!'

The match is also famous because it included SEVEN Arsenal men — Drake (centre-forward), Frank Moss (goalkeeper), George Male (right-back), Eddie Hapgood (left-back), Wilf Copping (left-half), Ray Bowden (inside-right),

BRAVE, determined and recklessly brave, Drake was one of the most feared centre-forwards in soccer.

and Cliff Bastin (inside-left). And Tom Whittaker was the England trainer!

Says Drake: 'Clearly Mussolini's directive had a lot to do with the do-or-die approach the Italians adopted that afternoon.

'From Frank Moss in goal with a badly damaged shoulder, to Eddie Hapggod who played on with a broken nose, most of us had bruises to remind us of the match.

'But we won it, and the side played well. In fact, before Italy knew what had hit them they were three goals down.

'Eric Brook and Cliff Bastin were deadly together on the left.

'I scored on my debut — a great moment to savour, and by the time we were three up — Eric scored the other two goals

DRAKE bursts through at Highbury to unleash one of his thunderbolts.

— Italy had decided to forget the ball and get on with the game!

'Of course we had some iron men in action as well. Wilf Copping never shaved on match days and his greyish blue stubble gave him a rather satanic appearance. His motto, in clipped Yorkshire accent, was: 'First man in tackle never gets hurt.'

'Wilf let the Italians know he was around when the going got tough yet he was hard and fair. He was never sent off or booked.

'Our mood was typified by Eric Brook. He had already scored a fine goal, then saw Italy's agile keeper save one of his piledriver penalty kicks. He was so amazed, he insisted on taking a free kick we were awarded shortly after. This time the ball sizzled home, and his grin was enough.'

The Italians claimed the injury to centre-half Monti, who played for both the Argentine and Italy in the World Cup, started the mayhem. He broke a toe early on and when he hobbled off after 20 minutes he claimed he had been deliberately fouled.

Drake will have none of that. He added: 'We paralysed Italy in the first 15 minutes. It was superb football and we couldn't play any better. We might have had five or six goals.

'It was this which caused the trouble. Only a few weeks before Italy had won the World Cup — from which we stood aloof in those days — and they came to show who were the masters.

'It was sheer frustration at being outplayed, and they lost their heads completely.

'Their keeper Ceresoli was accustomed to the continental habit — which has now spread here — of regarding the goalkeeper as a sacred cow. He was coming out unhampered to gather centres and then bouncing the ball at leisure until he felt like clearing.

'I was used to challenging the goalkeeper and even today the rules allow you to give him a fair shoulder charge.

'I got tired of the way he took his time in getting rid of the ball so I turned and challenged him. The next moment I was on the floor with three or four defenders around me and one with his arm around my neck, throttling me!'

It was the second international for England's slightly built 19-year-old outside-right, and his intention of not getting

DRAKE, the man you could always pick out in a crowd.

involved in the angry exchanges was so obvious that one newspaper claimed: 'He lacks the big match temperament.'

It was Stanley Matthews.

One other game Drake will never forget was the 1936 F.A. Cup Final against Sheffield United at Wembley. With less than 20 minutes left Alex James and Cliff Bastin carved out an opening for Drake to smash the ball left-footed into the United net for a 1-0 victory. He still gets vivid reminders of the game with a stabbing pain in his left leg. Drake had damaged it that season — needing a cartilage operation a few weeks after his seven goals against Villa.

He made his comeback a week before the Final — ironically against Villa, again scoring the goal which sent them down to the Second Division.

When Drake had a testimonial at Fulham where he eventually became chief scout, Villa sent a donation with this message: 'Never mind Ted — all is forgiven!'

Drake's career at Arsenal ended after he sustained a spinal injury in a wartime match at Reading in 1945.

He became manager at Elm Park and moved on to Chelsea

in 1952, steering them to their only Football League title in season 1954-55.

Drake now lives in retirement in West London. But his goals will never be forgotten at Arsenal.

Last, but not least, in this immortal quartet of 'Greats' from the Thirties comes EDDIE HAPGOOD, like Bastin, a West Countryman.

Hapgood brought new dimensions to full-back play — he was cultured, classy and thoughtful. Not for him the 'big boot' upfield that characterised so many defenders of his era.

Immaculately groomed on and off the pitch — he had a shock of black hair that immediately picked him out in a crowd — he was beautifully built, a long and accurate kicker of the ball, and his positional play and tackling were second to none.

For years he and George Male were the best club pair in England — a partnership that eventually led to them both being selected for the international side on numerous occasions.

Hapgood was a product of Bristol junior soccer and Rovers were the first club to take any notice of this cool young man who was playing left-back for St Phillip's Adult School Juniors.

Hapgood, 18, was given a trial at Eastville and made a big enough impression to be offered professional terms.

Rovers were prepared to guarantee him a first-team place and pay him £8 a week.

But they suggested he might like to earn his summer wages by driving a coal cart.

Shocked, he turned this down flat and took up an alternative offer from Kettering Town. Not that he was to last long there — after just 12 games he was spotted by Chapman who couldn't believe his luck. A fee of £1,000 — £750 down and a further £250 for a friendly match — was all that it needed to take Hapgood to Highbury and the start of one of the most distinguished careers in soccer.

THE classical Eddie Hapgood — not for him the big boot upfield.

That was 1928. He was to star in over 440 games for Arsenal before retirement in 1939 — winning five League Championship medals and playing in three F.A. Cup Finals.

He had six years as an England international (30 Caps) and his two proudest moments came, firstly, with the famous match against Germany in the Olympic Stadium in Berlin in 1938 when 100,000 fanatical fans saw the shamefaced England players give the hated Nazi salute (much against their will).

HAVE boots will travel! Eddie prepares for a big match, even in his overcoat.

It spurred the England team to destroy the pride of Nazi football on the pitch, winning 6-3.

In 1939 there was an equally memorable match with Scotland at Hampden Park, Glasgow when Hapgood captained England to victory with a Tommy Lawton goal minutes from time. Hapgood danced with joy on the pitch as the ball went in.

The only difficulty Hapgood had at Highbury in the early days occurred when he kept getting knocked out when heading the heavy, wet leather ball of the time.

What didn't help was that Hapgood was only 9st 6lbs and a vegetarian to boot!

EDDIE HAPGOOD, still in overcoat, in retirement. He won 30 England caps.

Then trainer Tom Whittaker persuaded him to eat steaks to build up both his strength and weight.

Not long after he joined Arsenal, Hapgood was burned quite badly in an accident. Whittaker built him a special protective leather harness to stop the burns rubbing all the time. It was proof of Hapgood's 100% commitment and loyalty to Arsenal.

Of all the Arsenal players, no one was more greatly affected by the death of Herbert Chapman. He looked upon the great man as a father figure.

When he quit soccer, Hapgood became trainer at Blackburn Rovers and then manager. Further spells at management took in Watford and Bath City but, although he had been an outstanding leader of men on the field, it never quite worked out for him in the boss's chair.

When he wrote his autobiography he called it: *Football Ambassador*. That is what he was — and that is how this proud man will always be remembered at Highbury.

ALEX JAMES'S PLAYING RECORD

	LEAGUE		F.A. CUP		F.L. CUP		EUROPE		TOTAL	
	App	Gls	App	Gls	App	Gls	App	Gls	App	Gls
1929-30	31	6	6	1					37	6
1930-31	40	5	3						43	5
1931-32	32	2	5						37	2
1932-33	40	3	1						41	3
1933-34	22	3							22	3
1934-35	30	4	3						33	4
1935-36	17	2	6						23	2
1936-37	19	1	4						23	1
	231	26	28	1					259	27

* James also played in 2 F.A. Charity Shield Finals.

SCOTLAND: 1930 v England, Wales, Northern Ireland; 1933 v Wales (4 caps).

CLIFF BASTIN'S PLAYING RECORD

	LEAGUE		F.A. CUP		F.L. CUP		EUROPE		TOTAL	
	App	Gls	App	Gls	App	Gls	App	Gls	App	Gls
1929-30	21	7	8	4					29	11
1930-31	42	28	3	1					45	29
1931-32	40	15	6	6					46	21
1932-33	42	33	1						43	33
1933-34	38	13	4	2					42	15
1934-35	36	20	4	1					40	21
1935-36	3i	11	7	6					38	17
1936-37	33	5	4	3					37	8
1937-38	38	15	3	2					41	17
1938-39	23	3	1	1					24	4
946-47	6								6	
	350	150	41	26					391	176

* Bastin also played in 4 F.A. Charity Shield Finals (2 goals)

ENGLAND: 1932 v Wales; 1933 v Italy, Switzerland; 1934 v Scotland, Northern Ireland, Wales, Holland, Czechoslovakia; 1935 v Scotland, Northern Ireland, Italy; 1936 v Scotland, Wales, Germany, Austria; 1937 v Wales, Northern Ireland; 1938 v Scotland, Germany, Switzerland, France (21 caps).

TED DRAKE'S PLAYING RECORD

	LEAGUE		F.A. CUP		F.L. CUP		EUROPE		TOTAL	
	App	Gls	App	Gls	App	Gls	App	Gls	App	Gls
1933-34	10	7							10	7
1934-35	41	42	4	1					45	43
1935-36	26	24	3	3					29	27
1936-37	26	20	3	7					29	27
1937-38	27	17	3	1					30	18
1938-39	38	14	1						39	14
	168	124	14	12					182	136

* Drake also played in 2 F.A. Charity Shield Finals (3 goals)

ENGLAND: 1935 v Italy, Northern Ireland; 1936 v Wales; 1937 v Hungary; 1938 v France (5 caps).

EDDIE HAPGOOD'S PLAYING RECORD

	LEAGUE		F.A. CUP		F.L. CUP		EUROPE		TOTAL	
	App	Gls	App	Gls	App	Gls	App	Gls	App	Gls
1927-28	3								3	
1928-29	17		4						11	
1929-30	38		8						46	
1930-31	38		3						41	
1931-32	41		6						47	
1932-33	38								38	
1933-34	40		4						44	
1934-35	34	1	3						37	1
1935-35	33		7						40	
1936-37	1	2							34	1
1937-38	41		3						44	
1938-39	38		1						39	
	393	2	41						434	2

* Hapgood also played in 6 F.A. Charity Shield Finals

ENGLAND: 1933 v Italy, Switzerland; 1934 v Scotland, Northern Ireland, Wales, Hungary, Czechoslovakia; 1935 v Scotland, Northern Ireland, Wales, Italy, Holland; 1936 v Scotland, Northern Ireland, Wales, Germany, Austria, Belgium; 1937 v Finland; 1938 v Scotland, Germany, Switzerland, France; 1939 v Scotland, Wales, Northern Ireland, Republic of Ireland, Norway, Italy, Yugoslavia (30 caps).

Arsenal Honours

Football League Division One
Champions: 1931 1933 1934 1935 1938 1948 1953 1971 1989
Runners-up: 1926 1932 1973

Football League Division Two
Runners-up: 1904

F.A. Cup
Winners: 1930 1936 1950 1971 1979
Runners-up: 1927 1932 1952 1972 1978 1980

League Cup
Winners: 1987
Runners-up: 1968 1969 1988

Fairs Cup
Winners: 1970

Cup Winners' Cup
Runners-up: 1980

Arsenal Facts

Season	P	W	D	L	F	A	Pts	Position
1929-30	42	14	11	17	78	66	39	14th
1930-31	42	28	10	4	127	59	66	1st
1931-32	42	22	10	10	90	48	54	2nd
1932-33	42	25	8	9	118	61	58	1st
1933-34	42	25	9	8	75	47	59	1st
1934-35	42	23	12	7	115	46	58	1st
1935-36	42	15	15	12	78	48	45	6th
1936-37	42	18	16	8	80	49	52	3rd
1937-38	42	21	10	11	77	44	52	1st
1938-39	42	19	9	14	55	41	47	5th
1946-47	42	16	9	17	72	70	41	13th
1947-48	42	23	13	6	81	32	59	1st
1948-49	42	18	13	11	74	44	49	5th
1949-50	42	19	11	12	79	55	49	6th
1950-51	42	19	9	14	73	56	47	5th
1951-52	42	21	11	10	80	61	53	3rd
1952-53	42	21	12	9	97	64	54	1st
1953-54	42	15	13	14	75	73	43	12th
1954-55	42	17	9	16	69	63	43	9th
1955-56	42	18	10	14	60	61	46	5th
1956-57	42	21	8	13	85	69	50	5th
1957-58	42	16	7	19	73	85	39	12th
1958-59	42	21	8	13	88	68	50	3rd
1959-60	42	15	9	18	68	80	39	13th
1960-61	42	15	11	16	77	85	41	11th
1961-62	42	16	11	15	71	72	43	10th
1962-63	42	18	10	14	86	77	46	7th
1963-64	42	17	11	14	90	82	45	8th

Season	P	W	D	L	F	A	Pts	Position
1964-65	42	17	7	18	69	75	41	13th
1965-66	42	12	13	17	62	75	37	14th
1966-67	42	16	14	12	58	47	46	7th
1967-68	42	17	10	15	60	56	44	9th
1968-69	42	22	12	8	56	27	56	4th
1969-70	42	12	18	12	51	49	42	12th
1970-71	42	29	7	6	71	29	65	1st
1971-72	42	22	8	12	58	40	52	5th
1972-73	42	23	8	11	57	43	57	2nd
1973-74	42	14	14	14	49	51	42	10th
1974-75	42	13	11	18	47	49	37	16th
1975-76	42	13	10	19	47	53	36	17th
1976-77	42	16	11	15	64	59	43	8th
1977-78	42	21	10	11	60	37	52	5th
1978-79	42	17	14	11	61	48	48	7th
1979-80	42	18	16	8	52	36	52	4th
1980-81	42	19	15	8	61	45	53	3rd
1981-82	42	20	11	11	48	37	71	5th
1982-83	42	16	10	16	58	56	58	10th
1983-84	42	18	9	15	74	60	63	6th
1984-85	42	19	9	14	61	49	66	7th
1985-86	42	20	9	13	49	47	69	7th
1986-87	42	20	10	12	58	35	70	4th
1987-88	40	18	12	10	58	39	66	6th
1988-89	38	22	10	6	73	36	76	1st

Arsenal's F.A. Cup Record

1929-30

Round 3	Chelsea	(h)	2-0
Round 4	Birmingham City	(h)	2-2
Round 4 (R)	Birmingham City	(a)	1-0
Round 5	Middlesbrough	(a)	2-0
Round 6	West Ham United	(a)	3-0
Semi-Final	Hull City	Elland Road	2-2
Semi-Final	Hull City	Villa Park	1-0
Final	Huddersfield	Wembley	2-0

1930-31

Round 3	Aston Villa	(h)	2-2
Round 3 (R)	Aston Villa	(a)	3-1
Round 4	Chelsea	(a)	1-2

1931-32

Round 3	Darwen	(h)	11-1
Round 4	Plymouth	(h)	4-2
Round 5	Portsmouth	(a)	2-0
Round 6	Huddersfield	(a)	1-0
Semi-Final	Manchester City	Villa Park	1-0
Final	Newcastle United	Wembley	1-2

1932-33

Round 3	Walsall	(a)	0-2

1933-34

Round 3	Luton Town	(a)	1-0
Round 4	Crystal Palace	(h)	7-0
Round 5	Derby County	(h)	1-0
Round 6	Aston Villa	(h)	1-2

1934-35

Round 2	Brighton	(a)	2-0
Round 3	Leicester City	(a)	1-0
Round 4	Reading	(a)	1-0
Round 5	Sheffield Wednesday	(a)	1-2

1935-36

Round 3	Bristol Rovers	(a)	5-1
Round 4	Liverpool	(a)	2-0
Round 5	Newcastle United	(a)	3-3
Round 5 (R)	Newcastle United	(h)	3-0
Round 6	Barnsley	(h)	4-1
Semi-Final	Grimsby Town	Huddersfield	1-0
Final	Sheffield United	Wembley	1-0

1936-37

Round 3	Chesterfield	(h)	5-1
Round 4	Manchester United	(h)	5-0
Round 5	Burnley	(a)	7-1
Round 6	WBA	(a)	1-3

1937-38

Round 3	Bolton Wanderers	(h)	3-1
Round 4	Wolves	(a)	2-1
Round 5	Preston North End	(h)	0-1

1938-39

Round 3	Chelsea	(a)	1-2

1945-46

Round 3 (1st leg)	West Ham United	(a)	0-6
Round 3 (2nd leg)	West Ham United	(h)	1-0

1946-47

Round 3	Chelsea	(a)	1-1
Round 3 (R)	Chelsea	(h)	1-1
Round 3 (R)	Chelsea	White Hart Lane	0-2

1947-48

Round 3	Bradford City	(h)	0-1

1948-49

Round 3	Tottenham Hotspur	(h)	3-0
Round 4	Derby County	(a)	0-1

1949-50

Round 3	Sheffield Wednesday	(h)	1-0
Round 4	Swansea Town	(h)	2-1
Round 5	Burnley	(h)	2-0
Round 6	Leeds United	(h)	1-0
Semi-Final	Chelsea	White Hart Lane	2-2
Semi-Final	Chelsea	White Hart Lane	1-0
Final	Liverpool	Wembley	2-0

1950-51

Round 3	Carlisle United	(h)	0-0
Round 3 (R)	Carlisle United	(a)	4-1
Round 4	Northampton Town	(h)	3-2
Round 5	Manchester United	(a)	0-1

1951-52

Round 3	Norwich City	(a)	5-0
Round 4	Barnsley	(h)	4-0
Round 5	Leyton Orient	(a)	3-0
Round 6	Luton Town	(a)	3-2
Semi-Final	Chelsea	White Hart Lane	1-1
Semi-Final	Chelsea	White Hart Lane	3-0
Final	Newcastle United	Wembley	0-1

1952-53

Round 3	Doncaster Rovers	(h)	4-0
Round 4	Bury	(h)	6-2
Round 5	Burnley	(a)	2-0
Round 6	Blackpool	(h)	1-2

1953-54

| Round 3 | Aston Villa | (h) | 5-1 |
| Round 4 | Norwich City | (h) | 1-2 |

1954-55

| Round 3 | Cardiff | (h) | 1-0 |
| Round 4 | Wolves | (a) | 0-1 |

1955-56

Round 3	Bedford Town	(h)	2-2
Round 3 (R)	Bedford Town	(a)	2-1
Round 4	Aston Villa	(h)	4-1
Round 5	Charlton Athletic	(a)	2-0
Round 6	Birmingham City	(h)	1-3

1956-57

Round 3	Stoke City	(h)	4-2
Round 4	Newport County	(a)	2-0
Round 5	Preston North End	(a)	3-3
Round 5 (R)	Preston North End	(h)	2-1
Round 6	WBA	(a)	2-2
Round 6 (R)	WBA	(h)	1-2

1957-58

| Round 3 | Northampton Town | (a) | 1-3 |

1958-59

Round 3	Bury	(a)	1-0
Round 4	Colchester United	(a)	2-2
Round 4 (R)	Colchester United	(h)	4-0
Round 5	Sheffield United	(h)	2-2
Round 5 (R)	Sheffield United	(a)	0-3

1959-60

Round 3	Rotherham United	(a)	2-2
Round 3 (R)	Rotherham United	(h)	1-1
Round 3 (R)	Rotherham United	Hillsborough	0-2

1960-61

Round 3	Sunderland	(a)	1-2

1961-62

Round 3	Bradford City	(h)	3-0
Round 4	Manchester United	(a)	0-1

1962-63

Round 3	Oxford United	(h)	5-1
Round 4	Sheffield Wednesday	(h)	2-0
Round 5	Liverpool	(h)	1-2

1963-64

Round 3	Wolves	(h)	2-1
Round 4	WBA	(a)	3-3
Round 4 (R)	WBA	(h)	2-0
Round 5	Liverpool	(h)	0-1

1964-65

Round 3	Darlington	(a)	2-0
Round 4	Peterborough	(a)	1-2

1965-66

Round 3	Blackburn Rovers	(a)	0-3

1966-67

Round 3	Bristol Rovers	(a)	3-0
Round 4	Bolton Wanderers	(a)	0-0
Round 4 (R)	Bolton Wanderers	(h)	3-0
Round 5	Birmingham City	(a)	0-1

1967-68

Round 3	Shrewsbury Town	(a)	1-1
Round 3 (R)	Shrewsbury Town	(h)	2-0
Round 4	Swansea Town	(a)	1-0
Round 5	Birmingham City	(h)	1-1
Round 5 (R)	Birmingham City	(a)	1-2

1968-69

Round 3	Cardiff City	(a)	0-0
Round 3 (R)	Cardiff City	(h)	2-0
Round 4	Charlton Athletic	(h)	2-0
Round 5	WBA	(a)	0-1

1969-70

Round 3	Blackpool	(h)	1-1
Round 3 (R)	Blackpool	(a)	2-3

1970-71

Round 3	Yeovil Town	(a)	3-0
Round 4	Portsmouth	(a)	1-1
Round 4 (R)	Portsmouth	(h)	3-2
Round 5	Manchester City	(a)	2-1
Round 6	Leicester City	(a)	0-0
Round 6 (R)	Leicester City	(h)	1-0
Semi-Final	Stoke City	Hillsborough	2-2
Semi-Final (R)	Stoke City	Villa Park	2-0
Final	Liverpool	Wembley	2-1 (after extra time)

1971-72

Round 3	Swindon Town	(a)	2-0
Round 4	Reading	(a)	2-1
Round 5	Derby County	(a)	2-2
Round 5 (R)	Derby County	(h)	0-0
Round 5 (R)	Derby County	Filbert Street	1-0
Round 6	Leyton Orient	(a)	1-0
Semi-Final (R)	Stoke City	Villa Park	1-1
Semi-Final	Stoke City	Goodison	2-1
Final	Leeds United	Wembley	0-1

1972-73

Round 3	Leicester City	(h)	2-2
Round 3 (R)	Leicester City	(a)	2-1
Round 4	Bradford City	(h)	2-0
Round 5	Carlisle United	(a)	2-1
Round 6	Chelsea	(a)	2-2
Round 6 (R)	Chelsea	(h)	2-1
Semi-Final	Sunderland	Hillsborough	1-2

1973-74

Round 3	Norwich City	(a)	1-0
Round 4	Aston Villa	(h)	1-1
Round 4 (R)	Aston Villa	(a)	0-2

1974-75

Round 3	York City	(h)	1-1
Round 3 (R)	York City	(a)	3-1
Round 4	Coventry City	(a)	1-1
Round 4 (R)	Coventry City	(h)	3-0
Round 5	Leicester City	(h)	0-0
Round 5 (R)	Leicester City	(a)	1-1
Round 5 (R)	Leicester City	(a)	1-0
Round 6	West Ham United	(h)	0-2

1975-76

Round 3	Wolves	(a)	0-3

1976-77

Round 3	Notts County	(a)	1-0
Round 4	Coventry City	(h)	3-1
Round 5	Middlesbrough	(a)	1-4

1977-78

Round 3	Sheffield United	(a)	5-0
Round 4	Wolves	(h)	2-1
Round 5	Walsall	(h)	4-1
Round 6	Wrexham	(a)	3-2
Semi-Final	Leyton Orient	Stamford Bridge	3-0
Final	Ipswich Town	Wembley	0-1

1978-79

Round 3	Sheffield Wednesday	(a)	1-1
Round 3 (R)	Sheffield Wednesday	(h)	1-1
Round 3 (R)	Sheffield Wednesday	Filbert Street	2-2
Round 3 (R)	Sheffield Wednesday	Filbert Street	3-3
Round 3 (R)	Sheffield Wednesday	Filbert Street	2-0
Round 4	Notts County	(h)	2-0
Round 5	Nottingham Forest	(a)	1-0
Round 6	Southampton	(a)	1-1
Round 6 (R)	Southampton	(h)	2-0
Semi-Final	Wolves	Villa Park	2-0
Final	Manchester United	Wembley	3-2

1979-80

Round 3	Cardiff City	(a)	0-0
Round 3 (R)	Cardiff City	(h)	2-1
Round 4	Brighton	(h)	2-0
Round 5	Bolton Wanderers	(a)	1-1
Round 5 (R)	Bolton Wanderers	(h)	3-0
Round 6	Watford	(a)	2-1
Semi-Final	Liverpool	Hillsborough	0-0
Semi-Final	Liverpool	Villa Park	1-1
Semi-Final	Liverpool	Villa Park	1-1
Semi-Final	Liverpool	Highfield Road	1-0
Final	West Ham United	Wembley	0-1

1980-81

Round 3	Everton	(a)	0-2

1981-82

Round 3	Tottenham Hotspur	(a)	0-1

1982-83

Round 3	Bolton Wanderers	(h)	2-1
Round 4	Leeds United	(h)	1-1
Round 4 (R)	Leeds United	(a)	1-1
Round 4 (R)	Leeds United	(h)	2-1
Round 5	Middlesbrough	(a)	1-1
Round 5 (R)	Middlesbrough	(h)	3-2
Round 6	Aston Villa	(h)	2-0
Semi-Final	Manchester United	Villa Park	1-2

1983-84

Round 3	Middlesbrough	(a)	2-3

1984-85

Round 3	Hereford United	(a)	1-1
Round 3 (R)	Hereford United	(h)	7-2
Round 4	York City	(a)	0-1

1985-86

Round 3	Grimsby Town	(a)	4-3
Round 4	Rotherham United	(h)	5-1
Round 5	Luton Town	(a)	2-2
Round 5 (R)	Luton Town	(h)	0-0
Round 5 (R)	Luton Town	(a)	0-3

1986-87

Round 3	Reading	(a)	3-1
Round 4	Plymouth	(a)	6-1
Round 5	Barnsley	(h)	2-0
Round 6	Watford	(h)	1-3

1987-88

Round 3	Millwall	(h)	2-0
Round 4	Brighton	(a)	2-1
Round 5	Manchester United	(h)	2-1
Round 6	Nottingham Forest	(h)	1-2

1988-89

Round 3	West Ham United	(a)	2-2
Round 3 (R)	West Ham United	(h)	0-1

Arsenal's League Cup Record

1966-67

Round 2	Gillingham	(h)	1-1
Round 2 (R)	Gillingham	(a)	1-1
Round 2 (R)	Gillingham	(h)	5-0
Round 3	West Ham United	(h)	1-3

1967-68

Round 2	Coventry City	(a)	2-1
Round 3	Reading	(h)	1-0
Round 4	Blackburn Rovers	(h)	2-1
Round 5	Burnley	(a)	3-3
Round 5 (R)	Burnley	(h)	2-1
Semi-Final	Huddersfield	(h)	3-2
Semi-Final	Huddersfield	(a)	3-1
			(agg. 6-3)
Final	Leeds United	Wembley	0-1

1968-69

Round 2	Sunderland	(h)	1-0
Round 3	Scunthorpe United	(a)	6-1
Round 4	Liverpool	(h)	2-1
Round 5	Blackpool	(h)	5-1
Semi-Final	Tottenham Hotspur	(h)	1-0
Semi-Final	Tottenham Hotspur	(a)	1-1
			(agg. 2-1)
Final	Swindon Town	Wembley	1-3 (after extra time)

1969-70

Round 2	Southampton	(a)	1-1
Round 2 (R)	Southampton	(h)	2-0
Round 3	Everton	(h)	0-0
Round 3 (R)	Everton	(a)	0-1

1970-71

Round 2	Ipswich Town	(a)	0-0
Round 2 (R)	Ipswich Town	(h)	4-0
Round 3	Luton Town	(a)	1-0
Round 4	Crystal Palace	(a)	0-0
Round 4 (R)	Crystal Palace	(h)	0-2

1971-72

Round 2	Barnsley	(h)	1-0
Round 3	Newcastle United	(h)	4-0
Round 4	Sheffield United	(h)	0-0
Round 4 (R)	Sheffield United	(a)	0-2

1972-73

Round 2	Everton	(h)	1-0
Round 3	Rotherham United	(h)	5-0
Round 4	Sheffield United	(a)	2-1
Round 5	Norwich City	(h)	0-3

1973-74

Round 2	Tranmere Rovers	(h)	0-1

1974-75

Round 2	Leicester City	(h)	1-1
Round 2 (R)	Leicester City	(a)	1-2

1975-76

Round 2	Everton	(a)	2-2
Round 2 (R)	Everton	(h)	0-1

1969-70

Round 2	Southampton	(a)	1-1
Round 2 (R)	Southampton	(h)	2-0
Round 3	Everton	(h)	0-0
Round 3 (R)	Everton	(a)	0-1

1970-71

Round 2	Ipswich Town	(a)	0-0
Round 2 (R)	Ipswich Town	(h)	4-0
Round 3	Luton Town	(a)	1-0
Round 4	Crystal Palace	(a)	0-0
Round 4 (R)	Crystal Palace	(h)	0-2

1971-72

Round 2	Barnsley	(h)	1-0
Round 3	Newcastle United	(h)	4-0
Round 4	Sheffield United	(h)	0-0
Round 4 (R)	Sheffield United	(a)	0-2

1972-73

Round 2	Everton	(h)	1-0
Round 3	Rotherham United	(h)	5-0
Round 4	Sheffield United	(a)	2-1
Round 5	Norwich City	(h)	0-3

1973-74

Round 2	Tranmere Rovers	(h)	0-1

1974-75

Round 2	Leicester City	(h)	1-1
Round 2 (R)	Leicester City	(a)	1-2

1975-76

Round 2	Everton	(a)	2-2
Round 2 (R)	Everton	(h)	0-1

1976-77

Round 2	Carlisle United	(h)	3-2
Round 3	Blackpool	(a)	1-1
Round 3 (R)	Blackpool	(h)	0-0
Round 3 (R)	Blackpool	(h)	2-0
Round 4	Chelsea	(h)	2-1
Round 5	QPR	(a)	1-2

1977-78

Round 2	Manchester United	(h)	3-2
Round 3	Southampton	(h)	2-0
Round 4	Hull City	(h)	5-1
Round 5	Manchester City	(a)	0-0
Round 5 (R)	Manchester City	(h)	1-0
Semi-Final	Liverpool	(a)	1-2
Semi-Final	Liverpool	(h)	0-0
			(agg 1-2)

1978-79

Round 2	Rotherham United	(a)	1-3

1979-80

Round 2	Leeds United	(a)	1-1
Round 2 (R)	Leeds United	(h)	7-0
Round 3	Southampton	(h)	2-1
Round 4	Brighton	(a)	0-0
Round 4 (R)	Brighton	(h)	4-0
Round 5	Swindon Town	(h)	1-1
Round 5 (R)	Swindon Town	(a)	3-4

1980-81

Round 2	Swansea	(a)	1-1
Round 2 (R)	Swansea	(h)	3-1
Round 3	Stockport County	(a)	3-1
Round 4	Tottenham Hotspur	(a)	0-1

1981-82

Round 2	Sheffield United	(a)	0-1
Round 2	Sheffield United	(h)	2-0
			(agg 2-1)
Round 3	Norwich City	(h)	1-0
Round 4	Liverpool	(h)	0-0
Round 4 (R)	Liverpool	(a)	0-3

1982-83

Round 2	Cardiff City	(h)	2-1
Round 2	Cardiff City	(a)	3-1
			(agg 5-2)
Round 3	Everton	(a)	1-1
Round 3 (R)	Everton	(h)	3-0
Round 4	Huddersfield Town	(h)	1-0
Round 5	Sheffield Wednesday	(h)	1-0
Semi-Final	Manchester United	(h)	2-4
Semi-Final	Manchester United	(a)	1-2

1983-84

Round 2	Plymouth	(a)	1-1
Round 2	Plymouth	(h)	1-0
			(agg 2-1)
Round 3	Tottenham Hotspur	(a)	2-1
Round 4	Walsall	(a)	1-2

1984-85

Round 2	Brstol Rovers	(h)	4-0
Round 2	Bristol Rovers	(a)	1-1
			(agg 5-1)
Round 3	Oxford United	(a)	2-3

1985-86

Round 2	Hereford United	(a)	0-0
Round 2	Hereford United	(h)	2-1
			(agg 2-1)
Round 3	Manchester City	(a)	2-1
Round 4	Southampton	(h)	0-0
Round 4 (R)	Southampton	(a)	3-1
Round 5	Aston Villa	(a)	1-1
Round 5 (R)	Aston Villa	(a)	1-2

1986-87

Round 2	Huddersfield Town	(h)	2-0
Round 2	Huddersfield Town	(a)	1-1
			(agg 2-1)
Round 3	Manchester City	(h)	3-1
Round 4	Charlton Athletic	(h)	2-0
Round 5	Nottingham Forest	(h)	2-0
Semi-Final	Tottenham Hotspur	(h)	0-1
Semi-Final	Tottenham Hotspur	(a)	2-1
			(agg 2-1)
Semi-Final	Tottenham Hotspur	(a)	2-1
Final	Liverpool	Wembley	2-1

1987-88

Round 2	Doncaster Rovers	(a)	3-0
Round 2	Doncaster Rovers	(h)	1-0
			(agg 4-0)
Round 3	Bournemouth	(h)	3-0
Round 4	Stoke City	(h)	3-0
Round 5	Sheffield Wednesday	(a)	1-0
Semi-Final	Everton	(a)	1-0
Semi-Final	Everton	(h)	3-1
			(agg 4-1)
Final	Luton Town	Wembley	2-3

1988-89

Round 2	Walsall	(a)	2-0
Round 2	Walsall	(h)	3-1
			(agg 5-1)
Round 3	Liverpool	(a)	1-1
Round 3 (R)	Liverpool	(h)	0-0
Round 3 (R)	Liverpool	(a)	1-2

Arsenal's European Record
European Cup

1971-72

Round 1	St't Drammen	(a)	3-1
Round 1	St't Drammen	(h)	4-0
			(agg 7-1)
Round 2	Grasshoppers Zürich	(a)	2-0
Round 2	Grasshoppers Zürich	(h)	3-0
			(agg 5-0)
Round 3	Ajax	(a)	1-2
Round 3	Ajax	(h)	0-1
			(agg 1-3)

Fairs Cup

1963-64

Round 1	Staevnet	(a)	7-1
Round 1	Staevnet	(h)	2-3
			(agg 9-4)
Round 2	FC Liège	(h)	1-1
Round 2	FC Liège	(a)	1-3
			(agg 2-4)

1969-70

Round 1	Glentoran	(h)	3-0
Round 1	Glentoran	(a)	0-1
			(agg 3-1)
Round 2	Sp Cb de Port	(a)	0-0
Round 2	Sp Cb de Port	(h)	3-0
			(agg 3-0)
Round 3	Rouen	(a)	0-0
Round 3	Rouen	(h)	1-0
			(agg 1-0)
Round 4	Dinamo Bacau	(a)	2-0
Round 4	Dinamo Bacau	(h)	7-1
			(agg 9-1)
Semi-Final	Ajax	(h)	3-0
Semi-Final	Ajax	(a)	0-1
			(agg 3-1)
Final	Anderlecht	(a)	1-3
Final	Anderlecht	(h)	3-0
			(agg 4-3)

1970-71

Round 1	Lazio Roma	(a)	2-2
Round 1	Lazio Roma	(h)	2-0
			(agg 4-2)
Round 2	Sturm Graz	(a)	0-1
Round 2	Sturm Graz	(h)	2-0
			(agg 2-1)
Round 3	Beveren Waas	(h)	4-0
Round 3	Beveren Waas	(a)	0-0
			(agg 4-0)
Round 4	FC Köln	(h)	2-1
Round 4	FC Köln	(a)	0-1
			(agg 2-2, lost on away goals)

UEFA Cup

1978-79

Round 1	Lokomotive Leipzig	(h)	3-0
Round 1	Lokomotive Leipzig	(a)	4-1
			(agg 7-1)
Round 2	Hadjuk Split	(a)	1-2
Round 2	Hadjuk Split	(h)	1-0
			(agg 2-2, won on goals)
Round 3	Red Star Belgrade	(a)	0-1
Round 3	Red Star Belgrade	(h)	1-1
			(agg 1-2)

1981-82

Round 1	Panathanikos	(a)	2-0
Round 1	Panathanikos	(h)	1-0
			(agg 3-0)
Round 2	Winterslag	(a)	0-1
Round 2	Winterslag	(h)	2-1
			(agg 2-2, lost on away goals)

1982-83

Round 1	Spartak Moscow	(a)	2-3
Round 1	Spartak Moscow	(h)	2-5
			(agg 4-8)

Cup Winners' Cup

1979-80

Round 1	Fenerbahce	(h)	2-0
Round 1	Fenerbahce	(a)	0-0
			(agg 2-0)
Round 2	Magdeburg	(h)	2-1
Round 2	Magdeburg	(a)	2-2
			(agg 4-3)
Round 3	IFK Gothenburg	(h)	5-1
Round 3	IFK Gothenburg	(h)	0-0
			(agg 5-1)
Semi-Final	Juventus	(h)	1-1
Semi-Final	Juventus	(a)	1-0
			(agg 2-1)
Final	Valencia	Heysel Stadium	0-0 (lost on penalties)